# MYSTIC OF THE HOLY WOUNDS

# MYSTIC OF THE HOLY WOUNDS

## THE LIFE AND REVELATIONS OF SISTER MARY MARTHA CHAMBON

*By the*
Visitation Sisters of Chambéry, France

*Translated from the French by*
Ryan P. Plummer

LAMBFOUNT
St. Louis, Missouri

**Published in 2019 by Lambfount · St. Louis, Missouri**
**www.lambfount.com**

Visitation Sisters of Chambéry, France, *Mystic of the Holy Wounds: The Life and Revelations of Sister Mary Martha Chambon*, translated by Ryan P. Plummer.

Originally published in French in 1928 by the Visitation Monastery of Chambéry, France, under the title *Soeur Marie-Marthe Chambon, religieuse de la Visitation Sainte-Marie de Chambéry, 1841-1907*. The original French edition bears a *nihil obstat* by Rev. François Bouchage, C.Ss.R., and an *imprimatur* by Archbishop Dominique Castellan of Chambéry.

ISBN 978-1-7328734-0-7

Printing and manufacturing information for this book may be found on the final page.

Cover image: sketch of Sister Mary Martha Chambon as remembered by her contemporaries, featured in book's original French edition.

# CONTENTS

# FOREWORD

*By His Excellency Archbishop Dominique Castellan*

THE prophets who announced the mystery of our Redemption, and the Apostles who preached it to the world, recognized the Holy Wounds of Our Lord Jesus Christ as the instrumental cause of our salvation.

"He was wounded for our iniquities: he was bruised for our sins. The chastisement of our peace was upon him: and by his bruises we are healed" (Isaias 53:5).

St. Peter repeats these same words (1 Peter 2:24) and St. Paul echoes him: It is by His Blood that we have been reconciled (Romans 5 & 6).

"What is more holy than these Wounds?" writes Pope Innocent VI. "It is from them that our salvation comes."

It is not surprising then that a poor country girl meditating on salvation should be struck by the importance of the Holy Wounds of Our Lord. It is entirely consistent with other mystical accounts that the Divine Master should recall to her the efficacy of these Holy Wounds for the conversion of sinners, for the fervor of contemplative souls, and for the obtaining of every grace.

The following work explains these essential truths. It is the life of a humble lay sister at the Visitation Convent in Chambéry,

*Mystic of the Holy Wounds*

the apostle of devotion to Our Lord's Holy Wounds, Sister Mary Martha Chambon.

The pious care, attention to detail, and desire for perfection with which these writings and memories were compiled are needless to mention. One will experience their charm.

The events of this cloistered existence are not many and, even less so, are they varied. It is especially fitting here to seek out examples of piety and virtue. As for the extraordinary gifts and revelations with which Sister Mary Martha was favored, one can admire them without aspiring to obtain anything similar. These are rare things and choice graces of which one should consider oneself most unworthy, even if one were to have purified one's soul by rigorous penances and continuously practiced Christian humility and patience.

It is also necessary to make an important distinction between Divine Revelation and the revelations made to certain souls throughout the course of Christian centuries. Divine Revelation was sealed by the final words of the last Apostle, St. John, finishing his Apocalypse and calling for the coming of the Sovereign Judge: "Come, Lord Jesus! Amen." Inspired Scripture thus completes Revelation. Its sacred deposit is confided to the Church and will no longer increase.

Other private revelations that might come do not ask of our intellects an assent of faith, but only a pious belief. What we learn from holy souls as the object of supernatural communications, and what they teach us or counsel us as having been transmitted to them by God, can add nothing new to the ensemble of revealed truths contained in Holy Scripture and recognized by the Church. The role of ecclesiastical authority consists in ensuring there is nothing in these private revelations that is contrary to the teachings of the Holy Books, but that everything is in accordance with the truth taught by the official organs of the Church and that we find in it grounds for edification.

It is having recognized these things that we willingly give our approval to this work. May the life of Sister Mary Martha make us better sense the love of God for men, the price of Our Lord's sufferings, and the fear of offending so august and tender a Majesty. This is the lesson of the Holy Wounds. We shall endeavor to follow in the footsteps of this humble soul. Hidden though she was, she will preach to us the love of prayer and work, and the spirit of obedience and submission, which are the true pathways to Heaven. The virtues are dearer than a ray of glory escaping the mystical openings from on high, for it is they that lead to the abundance of heavenly glory and happiness.

+ Dominique Castellan
Archbishop of Chambéry

# DEDICATION

## *To His Excellency Archbishop Castellan of Chambéry*

Your Excellency,

You expressed the desire to see appear the biography of the humble lay sister whose simplicity and innocence seem to have attracted the gaze of Our Lord.

Faced with this task, our inexperience confronted a difficult test. More than once, in order to sustain our courage, it was necessary for us—besides having the conviction we were producing a work useful to souls—to remember we were producing one pleasing to our venerable Father.

Allow us to dedicate to you this fruit of our obedience.

Studying closely the notes left by our Superiors, we saw the spiritual physiognomy of Sister Mary Martha Chambon take shape little by little. And what became more apparent to us each day was that—putting aside the extraordinary paths she had to follow—our lay sister was, above all, an "exemplary Visitandine."

Detached from the world, the Visitandine must live a life of intimacy and union with Jesus in "humility, meekness, and simplicity."[1]

---

[1] St. Francis de Sales, Conference 13.

Stripped of any personal ambitions, the Visitandine must have no other objectives than the love, glory, and interests of God. This is not only for herself; it is for souls that she has been chosen and called: "May all their life and exercises be for uniting them to God, and for assisting, by their prayers and good example, the Holy Church and the salvation of neighbor."[2]

These are things of which—following our Holy Founder— you love and excel at reminding us, Your Excellency, in each of your paternal visits, because you know it is our vocation, our "Mission."

This "Mission," our Sister Mary Martha, so unlearned and so simple, fulfilled wondrously, without interruption, from her religious profession to the grave, in constant intimacy with Our Lord, emphasizing His Holy Wounds.

She leaves us the continuation of this work.

We wish to do this by disseminating these pages in which each line proclaims so forcefully the love that, more powerfully than the nails, bound Our Lord to the Cross.

May your blessing, Your Excellency, give them greater strength and power; under your patronage, may devotion to the Holy Wounds radiate far and wide, for the good and salvation of the greatest possible number of souls!

Deign to extend this blessing over the humble family of Lémenc, so blessed by your paternal benevolence.

May it help us to become each day better Brides of Jesus Crucified, true sisters and heiresses of the Confidante of His Passion, true daughters of our Holy Father and Holy Mother, as

---

[2] Spiritual Directory, art. 1.

we are to Your Excellency by the profound respect, submission, and gratitude we place filially at your feet.

In the Heart of Him Whose place and authority you hold, we remain, Your Excellency, most humble, obedient, and unworthy daughters and servants in Our Lord.

The Superior and the Sisters of the Visitation of Holy Mary

God be blessed!

From our Monastery in Chambéry on September 14, 1928.

# PREFACE

THE letter of His Eminence Cardinal Gasparri that was placed at the beginning of the fourth edition of the booklet *Sister Mary Martha Chambon and the Holy Wounds of Our Lord Jesus Christ*, by providing us testimony of Our Most Holy Father Pope Pius XI's satisfaction, was an effective incentive and precious encouragement to carry through to completion the full biography of the Servant of God.

Sister Mary Martha is no longer an unknown. The leaflets and the little Notice on the Holy Wounds have carried her name to all parts of the world. Everywhere she seems to have been welcomed as a Messenger of Heaven. To everyone, she seems to have communicated the spirit of the apostolate that animated herself.

May Jesus Christ deign to bless those who, after her example, following in her wake, have themselves become apostles!

We are confident that the evangelization will continue with a scope and a fruitfulness that are enhanced by this new publication.

How much to learn from the humble nun in contemplating the Divine Wounds of Jesus, in listening to their eloquent voices, in placing one's sufferings and struggles in their sacred openings, and, lastly, in exploiting their infinite merits by offering them to God for the conversion of sinful souls and the ransom of those in Purgatory!

With the austere and loving lessons of Calvary will be mixed the sweet lessons of the Manger and of the Host—of the humble and silent life, interior and hidden, of which our Sister gives us the most perfect example.

What profit to keep company with this modest religious sister who thought herself so destitute but was so rich with Heaven's gifts! What messages to absorb from the divine lessons given her from the lips of her Master Jesus!

The events contained in these pages will undoubtedly appear extraordinary. They are. Just as the manuscripts of the Superiors reveal, the life of Sister Mary Martha was lived in habitual contact with Heaven.

However, taken in their totality and independently of any interpretation, these events present themselves to us with such a character of truthfulness that doubt seems forbidden to us.

We have the testimony of enlightened priests, officially tasked with the spiritual direction of the Community.

We have the testimony of our venerable Mothers Marie-Alexis Blanc and Thérèse-Eugénie Revel, who accorded their daughter a respectful trust and who, over the course of twenty years, at the invitation of ecclesiastical superiors, consigned in writing, with a painstaking care, the accounts obedience obtained each day from the humble lay sister.

We can add the testimony of the "contemporaries." The disclosure of the manuscripts was a revelation for our elder sisters. In reading these things of which they had been unaware, they see Sister Mary Martha come to life again before their eyes, and the things in her conduct and the gestures that might have puzzled them in times past now clearly explain themselves. In all of the expressions in which the "Master's teaching" was cloaked, they rediscover what sometimes escaped her in "scraps" in the course of her poor conversations as an unlearned woman incapable of expressing a lofty thought in complete and successive sentences.

As for issuing a judgment on the "divine communications," on their reality, extent, nature, or form, it would be presumptuous of us. And we disavow in advance any excessively affirmative, exaggerated, or erroneous expression that might escape from our pen. We have nothing to judge or debate. More modest and, at the same time, more consoling is our role:

To follow our well-beloved Sister throughout her existence, by bringing to light the memories of the Community and—to a larger extent—the notes of her Confidantes;

To organize these notes taken day to day and hastily jotted in twenty or so notebooks in the rare moments at a superior's disposal;

To try to relate them to some principal points and to show how the chosen one of Jesus was prepared, called, formed, and led by the Divine Master.

Such is our role, modest as we have said, and consoling… but sufficiently heavy for our weakness! We therefore thank with the most fervent gratitude those who gladly helped us with their advice.

One of our last superiors, taken too soon from her daughters, our Very Honorable Mother Jeanne-Françoise Breton, had in fact prepared the way for us. Right after Sister Mary Martha's death she composed a summary of her life, which has not left our archives, but has become for us a precious foundation and at the same time an authentic source of information, especially for the final years and death of our Sister. For our Very Honorable Mother speaks here as a primary and incontestable witness. It was she who closed the eyes of Sister Mary Martha. It was she who composed the beautiful prayer, cited elsewhere,[1] for asking the glorification of the Servant of God.

And we found, signed in her own hand in September 1907, a writing in which she offers herself to God as a "victim to continue [the work of] the dear deceased one."

May she, with our other former Mothers, help to complete the interrupted work by directing our pen, so that this publication of events to which they were witnesses and confidantes glorifies the immense mercy of the Lord towards His humble "plaything of love."

Our work will look little like ordinary biographies that proceed naturally according to a chronological ordering of events. Here, there are few external events: the outward life of Sister Mary Martha exhibits such a great uniformity—her personality fades so much into the obscurity that envelops her! Additionally, if the handwritten information brings to light the soul of our Sister, it does not provide any reference points allowing us to follow their progressive development. How, then, does one retrace the life of this soul without touching upon the supernatural in which she was constantly immersed? Upon examination, one discerns a triple life: an exterior life, an interior life, and a "mystical" life mingled with extraordinary events. All of these diverse aspects are so intertwined that one would not know how to dissociate them and recount them separately without distorting the physiognomy of the person: Sister Mary Martha moved about in the monastery performing the duties of her work; but at the same time, her soul remained in deep union

---

[1] See p. 278.

with God; moreover, she maintained constant relations with the Beyond; the invisible world of Spirits was as familiar to her as the material world. To us it thus seems best to not try to separate what appears to bring together the reality of things.

After the preliminary chapters concerning childhood, youth, and entry into religious life, our pages will primarily focus on the "mission" of Sister Mary Martha, with her fundamental devotion to the Holy Wounds, her other preferred devotions, and her virtues. Material that is rich in and of itself, and which also offers the advantage of presenting the details of our Sister's existence, in her milieu and in her comings and goings.

One might regret seeing costly diamonds embedded in a common mounting when they ought to be set in pure gold. They do not, however, lose their value. The poverty of our pious lay sister will better make stand out the richness of the divine voice that she believed herself to hear so often.

"My daughter, it is necessary to learn the simplicity of My words and not to change them," said our adorable Savior to His bride one day.

Our Very Honorable Mother Thérèse-Eugénie, to whom this message was transmitted, understood this no doubt as a warning for the notes she had to write concerning the graces granted to Sister Mary Martha. One senses she was scrupulously attentive to write word for word the innocent account of the dear Seer without adding anything. As a result, there is an almost total absence of personal remarks, which is regretful—a quick piece of information would sometimes cast so much light!

Without following her in every respect, since different is our task, we desire to at least imitate the perfect exactitude of this venerated Mother and, as much as possible, her reserve.

We hope thus to answer the desires of our Divine Master. And it will be a great joy for us to have contributed, in our own feeble way, to the fulfillment of this utterance from Jesus to His servant: "Your path is to make Me known and loved, especially in the future."

May Our Lord deign to grant us this grace, and may He be blessed!

From our Monastery in Chambéry,

September 14, 1928.

# CHAPTER 1

## SISTER MARY MARTHA'S
## CHILDHOOD & YOUTH

ISTER Mary Martha Chambon was born in La Croix-Rouge, a small verdant hamlet situated a few kilometers from Chambéry, amidst a magnificent landscape majestically overlooked by Mount Nivolet, with its superb cross which, since 1862, has projected its protective shadow over the entire region.[1]

The hamlet of La Croix-Rouge belongs to the parish of Saint-Pierre de Lémenc, the ancient *Lemencum* of the Romans. It was thus in this church adjoining our monastery—the former residence of the Feuillant Fathers[2]—that the child was regenerated, on the same day of her birth, March 6, 1841.[3] She received at baptism the name Françoise.

Our adorable Savior, who destined her for a perfect imitation of His states of humiliation, poverty, and suffering, imprinted upon her, from that first hour, the seal of His divine resemblance.

---

[1] A monumental cross piously erected by Count de Fernex on the highest point of Mount Nivolet at an altitude of 1,558 meters. A violent storm hurled it to the ground in 1910. The faith and love of the Savoyard people were immediately aroused. The ten thousand francs necessary for its re-erection were very quickly obtained through donations. With its present coating of aluminum, it sparkles anew in the light of the sun and blesses all of Savoy.

[2] For more information on the history of the monastery, see chap. 2, n. 7.

[3] The publication *Notice des Saintes Plaies* erroneously bears the date May 24, 1844.

This future bride of Jesus did not have a stable's manger for a crib; truly, though, the pitiful thatched-roof shack with a dirt floor, in which she came into the world, could rival the poverty of Bethlehem's grotto.

A single cold and damp room, this was the entire dwelling of the young Chambon household in its beginnings. When the family grew—for she was the eldest over one sister and six brothers[4]—some planks forming a midlevel loft served as a bunk area for the sons as they grew older.

In a cubbyhole, which was pretentiously adorned with the name of "stable," there was a goat—just one—that Françoise took to graze along the roads as soon as she was old enough. This memory of the little girl's is also linked to a sad one. One day when she was not paying attention, no doubt plunged in the thought of God, Who already made Himself felt in her soul, the mischievous animal left the thorny hedge for a neighboring field that was more appealing. At that very moment, the village constable had been passing by, and he mercilessly drew up a report. One can imagine the poor child's distress and the tears she cried in seeing her parents' already meager budget strained through her own fault. It was even believed among her family that this episode contributed in part to her deep disgust for the world, which she considered merciless and full of dangers.

The father of our little Françoise, a simple and upright man, had a lively faith and a certain piety. Healed by St. Philomena, he maintained a great devotion to her. He raised his family in a Christian manner.

He was, moreover, a hardy workman, always busy in the fields or in the neighborhood quarries. As they became old enough, his children followed him to work. With their father,

---

[4] One of them died in infancy. All the others preceded their sister in death.

they hired themselves out for the day, and in the meantime they also cultivated a small garden in front of their door.

The Chambon family's reputation was perfect. When the eldest son was considering marriage, since his future father-in-law had some property, friends were amazed to see him accept as a son-in-law a young man who owned absolutely nothing. "It is true that they are poor," answered this sensible man of faith, "but they are so good! The mother, especially, is such a fine woman, such a good Christian, that I am happy to give him my daughter."

Through honesty and hard work, the family rose from their poverty and attained a modest degree of comfort. They left the basement room—it presently functions as a cellar. Next to it they built a charming dwelling with a wooden balcony; the children fitted the rooms themselves. Sister Mary Martha would today see just how much the divine blessing has spread over those whom Jesus had promised to regard as His own: "Just as I will give the soul of the religious the hundredfold that I promised her, in the same way I will give it to your parents." That is to say, according to the Gospel, "the hundredfold in this world and eternal life in the other."

The mother of our dear Sister, who came from an impoverished branch of the noble Barandier family,[5] was truly

---

[5] Miss Louise B., an associate sister and benefactress of the monastery, one day learned of the illustrious lineage. Immediately, Sister Mary Martha rose in her esteem. She wanted to question her: "It would appear, Sister, that Your Charity is a descendant of the Barandiers… Wasn't your mother's name Barandier?"

"Yes, her name was Barandier."

"But you do know that is a noble family?"

"I didn't know… Oh, that doesn't mean anything… I don't pay attention to those things, ma'am," replied the good Sister, promptly fleeing the conversation.

worthy of these promises. Madame Chambon loved to take her little eldest one to religious ceremonies. She particularly loved going, accompanied by Françoise, to climb the Way of the Cross that was set up on the hill overlooking both the monastery and the city, and which, due to its topographic resemblance to Golgotha, bore the name "Calvary." She was a holy woman, according to everyone who knew her. Our Lord would one day show the child, after she had become His bride, the soul of this dear mother who delighted the Divine Heart with her deep piety: "This woman will have a very beautiful crown in Heaven."

Under such an influence, Françoise could only be turned towards God. She still recalled at the end of her life the joy of her innocent heart when her mother, tenderly placing her hand on the little girl's head at four or five years of age, said to a neighbor, "Oh, this one here, she will remain a virgin!"

The One Who is called "the Flower of the fields and the Lily of the valleys" would soon, in fact, draw to Himself this humble violet, whose such pure perfume was made to please Him. Let us leave our Sister herself to recount, as she did shortly before her death, in her rustic language and with delightful details about her upbringing in the Savoy countryside around 1850, the divine advances that were a part of her most distant memories: "My mother put the service of God before everything. She was strict with my brothers. She never gave them breakfast unless they had said their prayers. Sometimes they cried because they were hungry, but she did not give in. My father worked in the fields. He worked hard, he was good. I also had an aunt, my godmother. She was a good woman.

"One Good Friday—I was eight or nine years old—my aunt took me to venerate the Cross down below.[6] When I was

---

[6] Her gesture indicated the crypt of the Lémenc church, close to where the encounter took place.

kneeling, she told me, 'Françoise, extend your arms in the form of a cross and say five Our Fathers and five Hail Marys.' I had difficulty extending my arms because, shortly before, I had hurt my stomach when loading a bundle of hay. For several days, I was hardly able to eat anything... I was weak... I was unable to stand up... but I stretched out my arms and I said the five Our Fathers. At that moment, I saw Him for the first time! He was hanging on the Cross, all covered in blood, all torn open!... Oh, what a state He was in!... He said nothing to me. After a little while, my aunt took me away. I did not tell her that I had seen Him, not her or anyone."

This was the first revelation of the Savior's Passion, which was to hold such an important place in her existence.

Jesus did not speak to her. Does He need words to make Himself heard?... But undoubtedly an infinite power of attraction escaped Christ's adorable wounds and enkindled in this young soul the desire that consumed His own Heart: that of a more intimate union in His sacrament of love.

To go to communion! To receive Jesus! Françoise from then on had no other aspiration. When she confided this to the parish priest, he responded, "My little child, you have to learn your catechism."

"But my mother sent me to school, and I knew my catechism right away," she recounted, half-surprised and half-triumphant. It was believed a special grace had helped her, all the more so because this knowledge of the catechism was learned through hearing and her education was limited—Sister Mary Martha never knew how to read or write.

But how learned she already was, without suspecting it, in the knowledge of life and of Christian virtues! At this very tender age, she understood and had a proclivity towards mortification.

What is there, however, for such a poor little girl to sacrifice? The souls of children—when they are chosen souls, such as little Anne de Guigné—teach grown-ups a lesson in these matters. "Mother," Françoise would implore, "give me the soup before the butter is in it."

The little girl had been given a tiny corner in the humble cottage to place some images she had received. It was her altar. Each night, when she thought everyone was asleep, she would quietly get up and spend a long time kneeling on the bare floor, praying with all her young love's fervor, until the moment her mother would catch notice and tell her to go back to bed.

Sometimes during the day, Françoise would escape her mother's supervision and run next door to her godmother's.

This sister of her father's, who was unmarried, lived for an unknown reason in a former hermitage, an oratory or chapel, still surmounted by a miniature steeple with a small bell. The hamlet of La Croix-Rouge, quite distant from the parish church, certainly had need for this place of prayer. Perhaps in the wake of the Revolution the little abandoned chapel had been bequeathed to the pious woman. Whatever the case, she liked to bring parents and neighbors together inside her peaceful home to pray the communal rosary.[7] The "chapel," as it was still called, thus continued to serve its original purpose.

Françoise loved very much both the "chapel" and the good aunt, her godmother. We suspect that the godmother, in order to have had such attractive qualities, must not have been lacking in

---

[7] The rosary was recited before an antique gilded wooden statue of the Blessed Virgin that members of Sister Mary Martha's family recently donated to our Community in her memory. In an expression of touching faith, everyone gathered at the feet of the venerated image to pray one last time before saying their goodbyes, and there were tears in their eyes as they parted with it.

affection! Gladly she looked after her goddaughter. Gladly she took the place of the overburdened mother in taking the child to the church. The time having come, she carefully helped her to prepare for her first communion.

Finally, the great day came: September 8, 1850. Let us defer to the words of our dear privileged one recalling her memories as a young communicant many years later: "I then made my first communion… It was here in the church of Lémenc. And when I went to communion, it was the Child Jesus I saw and received… Oh, how happy I was!… He told me that each time I would go to communion it would be like this…"

"What did He look like, the Child Jesus?" asked her interlocutor. "Did he have little blond curls and a white robe like in the pictures?"

"Oh, my dear Sister," she interrupted, "it wasn't like that! We can't say those things, no?" She continued, "And since then, I have always seen Him!… Oh, it is Heaven! One has Paradise in their heart. You see, the good God has always spoiled me, but I was once told it is because I am poor and ignorant.

"We were always together. When I went to work in the fields or to gather grass for the goat, the Child Jesus was there close to me. We would go on the paths, we worked, we always came back together. I was happy! I sang…"

"And what did you sing?"

"The *Tantum Ergo*… everything sung in church. The priest often allowed me to go to communion. Sometimes it was the Blessed Virgin who gave me her Child Jesus. Once on the Nativity,[8] the Blessed Sacrament was exposed; after the high

---

[8] The Nativity of the Most Blessed Virgin, celebrated on September 8.

mass, I stayed and saw the Blessed Virgin. She had the Baby Jesus and gave Him to me. I don't know how long I remained in church, but when I returned home everyone had already eaten dinner. My father was angry, he scolded me for staying so long."

"Have you seen her again since then, the Blessed Virgin?"

"Oh yes, very often! But that time it was especially noteworthy."

Thus, from the dawn of her life we see two attractions that clearly stand out in the spiritual life of our Sister: On one hand, there are the Manger and the Eucharist, which she does not separate because it is always the Child Jesus that she sees in the white Host; the Manger and the Eucharist, that is to say the Holy Infancy and effacement. On the other hand, there is the Crucifix! That is to say suffering love, self-immolating love, atoning love...

In anticipation of so many graces, the soul of Françoise turned towards the contemplative religious life. And her personal inclination corresponded to the private sentiment of Fr. Lacombe, who had been the pastor of Lémenc since September 1859. But was it necessary to speedily direct a frail-looking nineteen-year-old girl to the cloister? Entry into the Third Order of St. Francis of Assisi in 1861 temporarily appeased her desire to consecrate herself to God.

Soon the desire reawakened, and it was more vehement than ever. Far from the attraction for God and divine things instilling in her a presumptuous assurance of her eternal salvation, this simple country girl—one can hardly believe it—feared being lost. Sometimes she experienced a terrible fear of hell. This fear, she later admitted, was one of the motives that led her to the cloister. She also felt she was called to make reparation for the defection of a family member who, lacking courage, had abandoned, after a few months, his vocation as a Brother of Christian Doctrine.

All while gathering grass and dead wood over the rocks around the walls of the Carmelite and Visitation monasteries—which did not yet have their ring of villas and gardens and could easily be gone around—the poor child did not cease to petition Our Lord to let her finally enter "in there."

"What did you want to do in the Convent," one of the sisters later asked her, "since you always had the Child Jesus with you?"

"I wanted to be occupied with Him only, to think only of Him, to live like the angels… and then to no longer see the things of the world, men, or anyone."

"But," smilingly responding, "you haven't seen much of the world."

"Oh, not much—my companions in La Croix-Rouge and a little bit of Chambéry."

In Carmel, where she was first presented, her strength was judged insufficient for the weight of the Rule. God had not marked her place there.

Fr. Lacombe then had the idea to propose his parishioner to our Very Honorable Mother Marie-Pauline Deglapigny. She was charmed by the girl's simplicity, encouraged her to wait until a place opened up among our lay sisters, and sent her away full of hope, although the latter was pained by this delay.

Françoise confided her cause to the Holy Souls in Purgatory, beginning a Stations of the Cross novena for them. The novena had not yet been finished when our Very Honorable Mother made known to her that she could enter. Sister Marie-Françoise Poulaz had just died.

That was in February of 1862.

Full of joy, the dear aspirant informed her mother that the doors to the Visitation had been opened to her. Let us listen to this innocent and living account:

"My mother was very happy, but a little upset as well, because I was the eldest and just really starting to work, but she was so Christian! 'You need to tell your father,' she answered.

"When my father arrived in the evening, I told him: 'Father, I am going to enter the Convent tomorrow. They are receiving me at the Visitation.' My father raised his hands to heaven, then let them fall to his knees: 'Oh, God forbid it, God forbid it!' he cried out.

"The next day I put my things in a kerchief and came."

"But your father?"

"Oh, right, my father, with his 'God forbid it!' He let me go."

What our Sister did not say, but which her family does remember, was that her departure was a great sorrow for everyone.

For her father, the words "Convent" and "Visitation" did not carry very specific meanings. They only signified separation forever! In order to spare him a painful episode, Françoise left without giving him a final goodbye, taking advantage of a moment when he was working in the fields. Hearing the train pass by and believing it was carrying away his child, the good man began to weep with all his heart, saying in his patois, which we translate: "My poor little one, I will no longer see you."

As for the mother, her pain was yet more profound. She cherished her eldest child with a love of predilection. She resigned herself, but she never got over the loss. Four years later, Mariette, the other daughter, went to join her sister. The generous mother did not make this new sacrifice without crying. But no complaints…

"The good God has taken them. If I had had six daughters, I think they would have all gone to the Visitation."

When our monastery opened its doors to her in 1862, Françoise was close to twenty-one years of age.

She was coming to fix her dwelling place at the foot of this "Calvary," whose paths she had so often traveled with her mother.

From the entrance, the miraculous Christ of our cloister, which had long ago illuminated St. Francis de Sales with its rays,[9] opened out its great merciful arms to her.

At the same time, valiant Christians were implanting the sign of the Redeemer in the towering rock of Nivolet.[10]

---

[9] The "miraculous Christ" was originally acquired by the Visitation of Chambéry in 1672. When St. Francis de Sales was visiting Chambéry during the Lent of 1606 and preaching in the now nonextant St. Dominic's Church at the request of the Senate of Savoy, a multitude of witnesses, including many of the city's most eminent personages, saw this same large wooden figure of Christ Crucified miraculously radiate light onto the holy bishop. See M. le Curé de Saint-Sulpice [André Jean Marie Hamon], *Vie de Saint François de Sales, évêque et prince de Genève: d'après les manuscrits et les auteurs contemporains,* 2nd ed., (Paris: Jacques Lecoffre et Cie, 1856) 1:541-542.—Trans.

[10] At the time of this translation in 2019, the Cross of Nivolet remains a familiar landmark to the people of Chambéry, still prominently situated on a mountaintop overlooking the city.—Trans.

A lover and future disciple of Jesus Crucified, Françoise was entering the convent under the auspices of the Cross, and beneath its shadow.

# CHAPTER 2

## THE VISITATION OF CHAMBÉRY

ONE would probably like to know about the religious community that had the good fortune to have Sister Mary Martha, the community to which she consecrated, with "her person and her life,"[1] the best of her affections.

"Our Blessed Father," St. Jane de Chantal wrote, "often expressed, both in letter and in speech, that he extremely desired the founding of this monastery in Chambéry because he foresaw its great fruits and usefulness for accomplishing God's glory and the salvation of souls."[2]

It was in response to this desire that one year after the death of St. Francis de Sales, the Venerable Mother de Chantal came in person to establish the new monastery, the sixteenth of the Order, on January 17, 1624. After twenty months of governing by the Saint, several of the first Mothers of the Institute successively took up its direction. Our Venerable Mother Marie-Jacqueline Favre[3] died a holy death in the monastery in 1637.

---

[1] Formula of religious profession.

[2] These words are found in the convent book's account of the foundation, written entirely by St. Jane de Chantal herself.

[3] Daughter of the renowned jurisconsult Antoine Favre and sister of the academician Favre de Vaugelas, she was interred in the vault under the sanctuary of the church, the construction of which was only beginning at the time. Thanks to the generosity of Madame Royale Christine of France, Duchess of Savoy, the construction of this church continued, as well as that

The preceding year (1636), the Visitandines were able to settle permanently in buildings constructed according to the plan in the Order's Customs.[4] They would live there until June 1793. Savoy at this time was undergoing the same fate as Revolutionary France,[5] and the forty religious who were living in the monastery under the leadership of the Very Honorable Mother Marie-Scholastique Bruni were violently expelled from their holy dwelling place.

The revolutionary storm passed, and religious houses were opened once again. And Divine Providence allowed our monastery to be one of the first that was reconstituted.

In 1806, an ordinance from Napoleon I authorized reestablishing the Daughters of the Visitation of Holy Mary, provided they devote themselves "to the education of young females."

It was thus, thanks to the measures of Fr. Bigex, the vicar general and future archbishop of the archdiocese, that the Visitation of Chambéry, under the appearance of a boarding school, was reconstituted on September 30, 1806.

The small core group that would give new life to the Community—formed by some Sisters from the old Visitation of Valence, who were subsequently joined by ten professed Sisters of Chambéry who had survived the turmoil, began under the

---

of the rest of the monastery. During the Restoration which followed the vicissitudes of the revolutionary era, the buildings and the church became the property of the Jesuits. Their college, built on the site of the old Visitation gardens, is today [in 1928] the *Lycée National*. [At the time of this translation in 2019, the school is known as *Lycée Vaugelas*.—Trans.]

Much to our regret, the excavations carried out in 1892 at the request of our community to find the remains of Mother Favre were unsuccessful.

[4] Located on the street currently known as Rue Jean-Pierre Veyrat.

[5] Present-day French Savoy did not permanently become part of France until 1860, when Françoise Chambon was nineteen years of age.—Trans.

leadership of the Very Honorable Mother Marie-Amédée du Noyer, who was superior of the first monastery in Annecy prior to the Revolution.

First established in a provisional home on Rue Saint-Antoine,[6] the religious then purchased the old Priory of Lémenc in 1808, which was nothing more than ruins at the time.[7] With Providence's funding and the Visitandines' toilsome contributions, working as laborers, new buildings went up little by little.

Words cannot express the abnegation our valiant "restorer" Sisters must have exercised during this era of reconstruction, and the amount of sacrificing that was their lot. It is with heartfelt gratitude that we read their story in our annals.

Their spirit of heartfelt charity and simplicity and their generous fervor in the service of God and of the Community were faithfully transmitted to a new generation, whose virtues the most senior among us were able to appreciate. The three

---

[6] The old Visitation Monastery, which had become the property of the Nation, was sold for a pittance on February 4, 1803.

[7] This priory, first started in 546 by two monks from the Benedictine Abbey of Ainay (in Lyon), was officially established in the eleventh century, with King Rudolph III of Burgundy and his wife Ermengarde as founders.

The Religious who built the church, which is today a parish church, called it St. Peter's. They would minister there until the seventeenth century, when they were then replaced by the Feuillant Fathers, a branch of the great Benedictine Order.

Presently [in 1928], a wing of our buildings leans up against the Lémenc church, while an interior courtyard and our gardens partially wrap around it. Framing the chevet is a grove of hazel trees over which towers a statue of the Sacred Heart, placed (in 1869) exactly opposite the tabernacle.

The Chapel of Our Lady of the Seven Sorrows, built in 1835 at the entrance of our little cemetery, is located a little further to the left.

These different places will be mentioned in the account of Sister Mary Martha's life.

venerable Mothers who welcomed Sister Mary Martha seemed to especially relive and embody these virtues. Their memory is too intimately connected with the Servant of God's for us not to give here an outline of their traits.

We have already named here the Very Honorable Mother Marie-Pauline Deglapigny.

She was an exceptional soul. Cardinal Billiet held her in such high esteem that he proposed her as a model to our Very Honorable Mother Marie-Alexis Blanc when she succeeded her as Superior in 1854.

Exceptionally good judgment, exquisite tact, admirable discretion, true humility, profound charity, and a sweet kindness united to a great firmness and ardent zeal for the observance— she possessed all the qualities that make for an ideal superior. It was she who received Sister Mary Martha and had her take the habit. Her name will resurface in the course of these pages.

Our Very Honorable Sister and former Mother Marie-Alexis Blanc was combining the office of Community Assistant with the duties of Directress[8] when Françoise Chambon was admitted to the novitiate.

One had to know this great soul to realize the good fortune of those religious formed in her school.

She entered the religious state at twenty-eight years of age. Hardly had she left the novitiate when the confidence of her superior had her return there as Directress.

Having an impeccable comportment, a penetrating eye, and "vivid" language, everything about her reminded one of Holy Mother de Chantal.

---

[8] Or Novice Mistress.

No one was less inclined, by nature, to be accepting of the extraordinary. In her eyes, as in those of our Holy Foundress, "it was a beautiful holiness to carry out the exact observance joyfully in the common life."

They liked to say that St. Peter, her baptismal patron, communicated to the soul of his "goddaughter" Péronne, the future superior, his ardent and active faith and his fiery zeal for the glory of God and the salvation of souls.

A strong woman in every sense of the word, she did not eat her bread in idleness—it seems God chose the times when she was in charge to multiply the building work as well as trials of all kinds.

Great was the esteem Archbishop Leuillieux, as well as his predecessors, had for the Very Honorable Mother Marie-Alexis Blanc.

"There is at the Visitation of Chambéry a superior who is a mistress of spiritual formation," said Fr. Cotton, the future bishop of Valence, and he sent three of his spiritual daughters to be formed by this hand.

Our dear Sister Thérèse-Eugénie Revel[9] had been devoting herself to the office of bursar when she was elected Superior in 1863.

She was also a model religious, a true pillar of observance. The formation she received from our Mother Marie-Alexis, whose novice she had been, left the imprint of moral strength on her naturally timid and very delicate soul. Her strength,

---

[9] A pupil at Sacred Heart in Chambéry, Azéline Revel was blessed in her childhood by St. Madeleine-Sophie Barat. After having fondly caressed her, the revered foundress advised, "Take good care of this little one, God plans to do something good with her."

completely imbued with meekness and humility, was rooted in the continuous presence of God, from which came an extreme receptivity to the movements of grace. "A religious must always be caught in an act of virtue"—this was her well-known and lived-out motto. We still regard her as the perfect example of the *Constitution on Modesty*.[10]

From 1863 to 1887, she regularly alternated every six years with our Very Honorable Mother Marie-Alexis in the offices of superior and directress. Both had been destined, in the mind of God, to become the guides, witnesses, and confidantes of the Savior's humble Privileged One. Both appeared to the Community to be hallowed by suffering and to emanate holiness.

Around these venerated Mothers was a living crown of honor and love, a gathering[11] of generous souls enamored of devotion and immolation, souls humble and childlike going straight to God like pure water to the ocean, making the monastery a sanctuary of recollection and, through the union of hearts, a cenacle of charity.

Poverty, this treasure of religious houses, was not lacking in the Community in 1862, no more than it had been during the heroic times of its founding and its restoration. It contributed, without a doubt, to nourishing fervor and holy dilatation in work.

We mentioned at the beginning of this chapter that there was a successful boarding school (of seventy to eighty students). This kept a portion of the religious hard at work and required the help of several domestic servant girls. It was among these latter,

---

[10] One of the constitutions St. Francis de Sales wrote for the Visitation Order.—Trans.

[11] A total of about forty religious, six of whom were lay sisters.

following the custom of the time, that Françoise Chambon took her place[12] in the house for an initial stage of a few months.

It was on August 2, 1862, that she, as a postulant, along with one companion of the same rank, crossed the threshold of the novitiate.

---

[12] February 1862.

# CHAPTER 3

## THE NOVITIATE & FIRST YEARS
## OF RELIGIOUS LIFE

THE joyous group of novices[1] cordially welcomed the new arrival. But no one, undoubtedly—seeing the rustic exterior and the extreme ignorance of Sister Françoise, to whom everything seemed so new—suspected the treasures contained in the soul of this young companion or the gift her person was to the Community.

The trained eye of the Directress saw deeper and more accurately. The postulant's humility and her ardent and profound piety had struck her from the beginning; and when, with the simplicity and spirit of faith that always characterized her, she little by little revealed herself to her, and at the same time the secrets of her innocent life and the attractions of grace with which the Lord was favoring her, Sister Marie-Alexis Blanc understood the underlying worth of the soul confided to her care.

The great docility of Sister Françoise, her total orientation towards God—the fruit of Heaven's solicitude—made easy, undoubtedly, her moral formation, which was assisted, if one may speak this way, by the Master's direct action. As for her getting used to the customs and work of the monastery, for

---

[1] Eight choir sisters and one lay sister who were already professed. One novice was to later become our very dear Mother Jeanne-Marie-Anne Spinella.

which her past life had so little prepared her, we believe it must have been hard.

Therefore, the beginning of her religious career was not without difficulties.

On certain days, mistakes and occurrences of forgetfulness and clumsiness were numerous. There were as many opportunities for the skillful Mistress to supply her new disciple with salutary humiliations. And since beneath the imperfection of the externals, her heart was not wanting in delicacy and her moral sensitivity was far from lacking, the young candidate sharply felt the corrections.

What was also very painful to her was the absence of her family. "My mind would always go there, to my parents," she later admitted to one of her companions, "but every time I realized it, I brought it back very quickly and put it in check…"

Furthermore, the fear of a possible dismissal tormented her: "I was so afraid of being dismissed. Think of it! I was so awkward… I didn't know how to do anything, not even the fire… There would always be smoke… Therefore, I was always saying, 'My good Jesus, keep me! O my good Jesus, please keep me!'"

The sheer good will of Sister Françoise and her generous efforts earned her the grace to proceed to Investiture. On April 29, 1863—after nine months of postulancy—she received, with the white veil, the name of Mary Martha—so appropriate for someone who would unite an interior life of rare intensity to unceasing daily labor.

The ceremony was presided over by Canon Gros, the future Bishop of Tarentaise, who at the time was the Vicar General of Chambéry and Superior of the Community. In an allocution full of piety and tender devotion, Father Lacombe, the Pastor of Lémenc, expounded on the happiness of the religious state, the grace of corresponding to this call, and the sublimity of the duties of our holy vocation.[2]

Fifteen months later,[3] on August 2, 1864, the Feast of Our Lady of the Angels, Sister Mary Martha bound herself irrevocably to Jesus through religious profession. She was twenty-three years old.

What happened at that hour of "everlasting benediction"[4] between the Heart of God and that of His Servant? Nothing of it came to light in either our Sister's conversations or in our Mothers' manuscripts. In light of the preceding graces and the superabundance of those that were to follow, it seems impossible that the Divine Bridegroom would not have lavished upon her some of these liberties with which He was accustomed in her regard. But the "secret of the King" was jealously guarded. Without daring to condemn this reserve, we confess that we regret it.

Mary Martha's companion in the taking of the habit, our good Sister Marie-Jacqueline Arbet, made her holy vows at the same time. A touching and unchanging union was established between these two souls of prayer and lasted as long as they lived. It was a charity full of respect and admiration on the one hand and of confidence on the other.

What clumsiness atoned for, and what services rendered by the dear "twin of profession"! And, in exchange, what simple growth on the part of the Lord's Privileged One!

---

[2] Annals of the monastery.

[3] Under the governance of our Very Honorable Mother Thérèse-Eugénie Revel, who was elected Superior in June 1863.

[4] St. Francis de Sales, wishes in the Book of Vows.

Many years later, when walking became almost impossible for Sister Marie-Jacqueline, it was in her infirmary cell that intimate and pious conversations took place between the two soul sisters, from which each one drew profit and consolation.

Sister Mary Martha, so discreet and closed vis-à-vis the Community, seemed to have made one exception in her companion's favor and confided to her more than one secret. Therefore, after her death, Sister Marie-Jacqueline—who would follow her to Heaven soon afterwards—often said, not without making us smile: "You will see, Sisters, you will see, she will be *worse* than Blessed Margaret Mary!"[5]

After her religious profession, Sister Mary Martha was still part of the novitiate for several years.[6] She therefore stayed under the direction of the Mistress of Novices, and even though, from this point forward, she had been appointed to the boarding school, where she spent her days, somewhat on the peripheries of the Community, she went each day, according to the Rule, to attend instructions and to receive counsel and monitions from the Directress.

What did she do during this time? There are very few documents. It is not impossible, however, by using the manuscripts and bits of information from the Elders, to evoke

---

[5] St. Margaret Mary Alacoque was not canonized until 1920, which is why she was only referred to as "Blessed" at the time.—Trans.

[6] Until 1869. At the Visitation, the novitiate continued for a few years after the profession that occurred upon completion of a one-year probation. Sister Mary Martha's novitiate was extraordinarily prolonged. We find the reasons for it mentioned in the manuscripts. Besides the greater ease our Mothers thus had to converse with the young Professed, they considered the presence of the dear Privileged One in the midst of the small flock to be a grace. (The alleged need for a more laborious external formation covered the true motives.) Similar reasons would motivate them to keep her in charge of the boarding school refectory.

with a certain fidelity the physiognomy of our Sister at this time of her existence. And this is yet another opportunity to admire the divine ways.

She did not stand out for any external attractiveness or for any gifts of the mind, this religious whom Jesus was going to surround with so much love and inundate with such brilliant lights. At first sight, as we know, nothing was predisposed in her favor: a total absence of intellectual formation; a memory and imagination that were quite mediocre; rustic manners and language, which at times amused people... when not making them impatient! Let us add a lively temperament and a somewhat tenacious will which, combining with the narrowness of certain views and notions typical among village people, suffice to explain imperfections she never succeeded in completely uprooting and which God used to conceal His activity in our humble Sister.

When in her touching simplicity she complained to Our Lord, "My good Jesus, with all of Your graces, You leave me all of my defects," He answered her, "Your imperfections are the greatest proof that what is happening in you comes from God. I shall never take them from you—they are the covering that hides My gifts. You desire so much to be hidden. I desire it even more than you."

"It is consoling to think," wrote a person of the world on this subject, "that one can love the good God and be pleasing to Him while having defects humiliating for oneself and trying for others."

Sister Mary Martha's defects did not prevent her from loving the good God, or even from loving Him much. Faithful to all of her duties, modest, silent, and recollected, the young Professed had as a distinctive trait a great devotion to the Passion of the

Savior. She had wanted to make a Holy Hour each day and very often asked this permission from her Mistress. The latter, who had already seen the efficacy of the humble child's prayers on the Heart of God, gladly granted her this favor. If she was sometimes refused, Sister Mary Martha did not insist and docilely withdrew. This docility was the Directress's consolation and what she loved to give the Sisters in the novitiate as an example.

These defects also did not prevent her from loving her Sisters tenderly or from enjoying their company.

On days of general leisure, she gladly participated in the communal merriment. Often her innocent mistakes even contributed to it.

To one of her companions, who wanted to be informed about a lesson she was unable to attend, she explained: "Sister, the preacher said, 'If you do not have charity, you are only a clanging sandal.'" Her vocabulary did not distinguish between "clanging sandal" and "clanging cymbal," which in her mind equally meant "worthless"!

Another time, as a Sister of remarkable artistic talent was being spoken of, Sister Mary Martha exclaimed in astonishment, "What, I thought she was a *writer-ette*! So then, she's a *painter-ess*!"

Like a child, she loved to laugh, and she expressed regret when she had to absent herself from an hour of merriment, unable to be "with the companions and as the companions."

One day, however, she did not appear at all for fear of offending our eyes. A young Sister had told her jokingly that she was not beautiful! "But this isn't news, Sister Mary Martha… You didn't know this?"

"Oh yes, how I know it. But you understand, it's not pleasant to hear it said. Ah, little Sister, little Sister who is teasing Sister Mary Martha!"

Certainly, the beauty of this daughter of the King was not on the exterior. But if God had treated her sparingly in certain respects, the Master of all gifts had reserved for Himself magnificent compensations. One would make note here of these features, struck with infallible signs which reveal the Divine Artist, and reveal Him all the more since the disgraces of nature did not disappear. In this intellect that was so unrefined, what lights and what profound insights! In this heart without a natural education, what innocence, what faith, what piety, what humility, and what thirst for sacrifice!

Sister Mary Martha's innate simplicity, desired by God, permitted Him to better reveal Himself to her gaze, which was free of all worldly knowledge.

After having read the *Notice on the Holy Wounds*, a serious-minded soul signed up for the full biography of the Servant of God and gave the following reason: "It is just that in your Sister I do not find poetic flowers or metaphorical narratives. I seem to be reading the great Saints of the past, bringing us the richness of practical and incontestable revelations capable of saving the world—a Gertrude, a Catherine of Siena, a Margaret Mary."

Indeed, we rediscover the words—which are sometimes even identical—of Our Lord to His great privileged ones. Inadvertently, one then remembers the physiognomy of our pious Lay Sister and one is struck by the extreme contrast that exists between her uncultivated intellect and her sometimes such profound intuitions! These words from the Gospel spontaneously come to mind: *Thou hast revealed them to little ones!*

O my God, it is to the little ones, to the simple, that You reveal Yourself!

# CHAPTER 4

## THE FIRST MANIFESTATIONS

OUR Very Honorable Mother Thérèse-Eugénie Revel had hardly begun her second three-year term when, on the Vigil of Pentecost, May 19, 1866, she saw our late Sister and former Mother Marie-Pauline Deglapigny pass away in her arms.

Close to her deathbed, the Community held itself in prayer. The final moment was approaching. All of a sudden, the dying one, inclining towards the young Mother, cast upon her a long gaze of ineffable tenderness which seemed to communicate to her: "Do not be afraid, I will be with you, and from Heaven I will be helping you!" Our Very Honorable Mother always believed she saw the effect of this maternal protection in the graces with which the Savior favored our Community in the person of Sister Mary Martha.

Throughout the two years following her profession, nothing striking had marked our Sister's plain and simple interior path. Aside from an uncommon gift of prayer, an ever-growing hunger and thirst for God, and a habitual recollection, there had been nothing truly singular that would foreshadow extraordinary paths.

However, shortly after this death, in June 1866, the young Lay Sister, who was just entering her twenty-sixth year, began to be favored with frequent visits from Our Lord, to which were also joined those of the Most Blessed Virgin, the Souls in Purgatory, and the Blessed Spirits.

"She enjoys the vision of God," the Very Honorable Mother Thérèse-Eugénie Revel would note a few months later. "At every moment she maintains a sweet commerce with Our Lord, His Holy Mother, our Holy Founders, the Angels, and the Saints. God the Father Himself has brought His infinite greatness down to her several times, giving her Jesus, illuminating her heart with heavenly lights."

At the same time were made known the initial demands of Jesus Christ, Who seemed to want to lead her on an extraordinary path.

Sister Mary Martha was first invited by Our Lord to spend nights stretched out on the floor of her cell. She opened up about this to her Mistress, who refused permission because the thing was outside of the ordinary rules. Our dear Sister humbly obeyed. Let us even say that she was not without experiencing a natural satisfaction from this refusal. But Jesus manifested His displeasure by withdrawing from that point forward all sleep from her whom, in His love, He had chosen as a victim.

After a long trial, our Very Honorable Sister Marie-Alexis Blanc did not believe she ought to oppose what truly appeared to be the Divine Master's desire: she granted the requested permission. "Sleep immediately returns, good and peaceful like that of a child!"

Shortly thereafter, it was a rough hair shirt that Sister Mary Martha had to wear day and night. A new hardship, a new manifestation of the Divine Will! The Directress sometimes ordered her to dispense with it—our docile child quickly obeyed, and joyfully, for she could only bear the hair shirt with difficulty. The Sovereign Master then compensated by sending His bride such great sufferings that one was forced to yield to His demands.

Then came the retreat of September 1866. Ever more engaging Sister Mary Martha on this penitential path, Jesus asked her to wear a crown of thorns on her head when she was lying on the floor at night with her arms outstretched in the form of a cross, in order for her to become His living image.

In response to such an extraordinary request, our Mothers hesitated a long time. Thus, there were new sufferings for our young Sister: unbearable headaches, astonishingly abundant perspiration, and universal pains. They were obliged to put her in bed. For several days, she took neither drink nor food.

One afternoon our Mother went to the sick one and asked her the cause of her state. Timidly, with a sorrowful expression, the poor child responded, "Your Charity does not want to permit what He desires."

"Is this regarding the crown of thorns?"

"Yes, Mother."

"Well! If it is truly Our Lord who requires this new kind of mortification from you, we must have a sign to recognize His Will… Let your perspiration stop immediately, your pains go away, and a perfect health be given to you this very hour. If this grace is granted to you and lasts eight consecutive days, we will believe God wants it and we will permit you to wear this crown."

"I went away," continued our Mother, "very emotional about what I had just done, and I went to Vespers, the bells for it ringing. Immediately afterwards, returning to the infirmary, what a surprise for me to find Sister Mary Martha up and eating with a very good appetite!"

"Who let you get up like this?" I exclaimed, not without some intensity.

"But, Mother, Your Charity ordered me to ask Our Lord for my healing. I did so, and He said, 'Yes, everything you want.' The perspiration stopped right away; all the pains disappeared. I got up, and I am so hungry! And I hope, Mother, that Your Charity will still let me have supper this evening… What must I do now?"

She was in perfect health the entire week, except for Friday, when she suffered a little. Regarding the condition our Very Honorable Mother made, the Divine Master responded, "My daughter, this day is consecrated to My sufferings, you must grant Me something."

It was no longer possible to resist the Divine Will, which was so clearly made known. Our Lord Himself taught His bride how she was to weave this crown with very sharp thorns, which no longer permitted her to lay her head down without experiencing sharp pains.

"Truly similar to a virgin martyr," wrote our Mother Thérèse-Eugénie, "she spent every night lying on the ground, her arms outstretched in the form of a cross, and her head encircled with a crown of thorns."

"On one evening when it seemed she could no longer bear the suffering, she complained about it to her Beloved. 'My daughter, push it in even harder,' He told her. Sister Mary Martha obeyed, and her obedience, as simple as it was courageous, received its immediate reward: all pain disappeared at that very instant.

For the penitential life God required of His servant, it was necessary to have extraordinary support.

On Holy Thursday, April 18, 1867, Our Lord had her ask her Superiors for the grace of daily Communion. They judged it good to permit her this.

This favor was so rarely granted at the time that, all while delighting in her good fortune, Sister Mary Martha felt herself covered in confusion, in the thought that all of her Sisters deserved this much more. She was also tormented by the fear of being outside the Rule and of drawing attention to herself.

However, Jesus did not cease the divine pursuits of His love. Not content having the nights spent on the ground with the hair shirt and the crown of thorns, in May 1867, He demands from our dear Sister the sacrifice of sleep itself, asking her, while everyone is asleep in the monastery, to keep vigil before the Most Blessed Sacrament.

Absolute Master in all things, He made her to understand that, if she was not given this permission by her Superiors, He would withdraw the special blessing of health He was then spreading over our boarding school.

After having granted her this permission for a few days, the Sister Directress believed she ought to order her novice to take a night of rest. On the next day, six of our students were sick.

Worried about them, our Mothers gave full liberty to our Sister. They did even better than that: they sided with the Divine Master in defiance of their own inclinations and against the temptations of their child.

When Sister Mary Martha, overcome with fatigue and sleepiness, would go to the evening "Obedience"[1] to implore

---

[1] At 8:30. The "Obedience" is a regular exercise that brings together all the religious twice a day to receive orders or recommendations from the Superior. It is at this time that they also ask for permissions.

them to send her to sleep, appealing to their natural compassion and human prudence, they would personally escort her to the tribune.

With such demands, nature is barely tended to. But is this not the normal price for divine favors? In the silence of the nights, Our Lord communicated Himself to His Servant in the most wondrous fashion. At times, undoubtedly, He left her to painfully struggle for long hours against fatigue and sleep. But more often than not, He would immediately take hold of her and transport her into a kind of rapture, in which He would instruct her all while transforming her.

His hold on this most humble, most simple, and most docile soul was growing each day.

# CHAPTER 5

## THE SPIRITUAL DIRECTORS

IN entrusting His Privileged One to our Mothers Thérèse-Eugénie and Marie-Alexis, God had chosen well. He knew how their fidelity would rise to the occasion in the trials awaiting them. He above all knew their spirit of faith, their prudence, and their humble submission to ecclesiastical superiors.

Very quickly, Sister Mary Martha's Directress and Superior felt they could not completely assume responsibility in leading this soul. True daughters of the Holy Church, they submitted the case to the priests who were the official directors of the Community at the time: Canon Bouvier, the Vicar General Fr. Mercier, and Fr. Ambroise, a Capuchin.

The archdiocese has not forgotten these three remarkable priests. As for the Visitation of Chambéry, it owes them a word of gratitude.

Canon Bouvier—"the Angel of the Mountains," as people liked to call him in Chambéry—was confessor to the Community for thirty-two years, from 1852 to 1885.

There is not a more beautiful eulogy than that of *La Semaine Religieuse*,[1] in the obituary announcing his death to the

---

[1] *La Semaine Religieuse de la Savoie* was a weekly newspaper published by the Archdiocese of Chambéry.—Trans.

archdiocese: "Canon Bouvier had a hunger and thirst for the glory of God and the salvation of souls. That was his single thought, his sole ambition. Therefore, he did not understand how one could make him a banal and purposeless visit, how one could come to him seeking something other than light amidst doubts, counsel amidst life's perplexities, a consolation amidst sadness, God's forgiveness and peace of soul after the failings of human nature."

And no one was in a better position than he to give those things—to his many years of experience were joined the piety of a holy priest and the erudition of a reputed theologian. He therefore inspired such a perfect confidence that a portion of the clergy had recourse to him and even his bishops entrusted to him the direction of their consciences.

The Holy Curé of Ars, on more than one occasion, said to people from Savoy who had gone to consult him: "Why are you coming here? Don't you have the Chaplain of the Visitation in Chambéry?"

Fr. Bouvier was privy to all the graces granted to Sister Mary Martha, for our Mothers did not do anything without his counsel and approval. But out of an extreme prudence and being foremost a lover of peace, he always maintained a great reserve in these judgments and assessments, deferring to the Superior, Canon Mercier, regarding anything proceeding from the internal forum of conscience.

Personally, however, his mind was made up on the matter. He believed in our Sister's supernatural path. We have clear proof of this in correspondence that was passed on to us after the death of its fortunate addressee. This correspondence, very regular for sixteen years, from 1867 to 1883, while shedding light on the motives that had kept a discreet silence about so many things for a long time, revealed in each line the mindset of our confessor. "I know," he wrote, "a soul with whom Jesus communicates. In the course of the week, I will recommend your affair to her. Speak nothing of this, this is absolutely secret; but the thing is very certain.

"The person is a person of great simplicity, consecrated to God through the vows of religion. Her manner of living is almost a continuous miracle. But impossible to give you further details—it is understood that if she comes to be known, the Divine Savior will take her from this world. She is on the usual path of the Saints."

Fr. Bouvier's conviction was so profound that he did not hesitate to entrust the intentions of Madame N. to Sister Mary Martha and to await the responses she would receive for her from Our Lord.

As for our Sister, not wanting to give her name away, he ordinarily referred to her by the expressions "our holy soul" and "our little saint." No one was in a better position to make an informed judgment.

Canon Mercier was the pastor of *Notre-Dame* in Chambéry when his relationship with the Visitation began.[2] In 1830, he merited a special right to our gratitude by returning the miraculous Christ[3] to our Mothers, a precious treasure kept in his church since the time of the Revolution.

He subsequently became Vicar General and, in the month of May 1867, replaced as Superior of our Community Father Gros, who was appointed Bishop of Tarentaise.

---

[2] A sister of Canon Mercier was a religious in our monastery named Sister Marie-Fortuné.

[3] See chap. 1, n. 9.

More than thirty-seven years of ministry, during which he was the object of trust of his bishops and of the archdiocese, would inspire in our Mothers the most perfect sense of security. We have always heard him spoken of in a tone of profound veneration.

As for Fr. Ambroise, a longtime provincial and dedicated to apostolic ministry for close to sixty years, his memory remains alive in all of Savoy.

The *Necrology* of the Capuchin Fathers gives him this strong, sober, and very laudatory appraisal: "Fr. Ambroise received the qualities that make men excel in governing their peers and in managing affairs. Endowed with a fine intellect, prudent by nature even prior to being so through experience with men and things, studying situations before acting, never leaving a difficulty without a solution, upright, never seeking detours, impartial and knowing only duty—in all things calm, a master of self, and wondrously self-controlled…"

The Visitation had the benefit of having him as a preacher for several outstanding retreats, and as an extraordinary confessor for the Community. He was kept informed about all important business and was often consulted by our Superiors. One fact shows the interest he had in Sister Mary Martha and the importance he gave to her communications: a precursor of the present movement, Fr. Ambroise had the *Invocations to the Holy Wounds* printed in Grenoble prior to 1880.

It was these three priests to whom our Mothers had recourse, qualified on account of their erudition, virtue, experience, and offices.

Besides their duties putting them into contact with Sister Mary Martha in the internal and external fora, they had in their hands the notebooks in which the accounts were written down day to day.

The examination was long, serious, and comprehensive. Our Sister was found to have all the guarantees that give security in these delicate matters: a spirit of humility, obedience, an enduring fear of delusion, a thirst for the communal life, and suffering for being excluded from it. The three examiners agreed that the path Sister Mary Martha was traveling bore the "divine stamp." Their conclusions confirmed the thinking of our Very Honorable Mother Thérèse-Eugénie Revel, which was summed up in the following attestation: "Obedience is everything to her. The simplicity, the honesty, the spirit of charity that animate her, her mortification, and above all her sincere and profound humility, seem to us the surest guarantees of God's conduct over this soul. The more she receives, the more she enters into a true contempt for herself, being almost always crushed by the fear of being in delusion. Docile to the counsel given her, the words of the Priest and of the Superior have a great power to put her at peace. What especially reassures us is her passionate love for the hidden life, her insistent need to escape all human notice, and the dread she has that what happens in her might be perceived."

All three advised continuing to write down the communications Sister Mary Martha would state she received from Our Lord. At the same time, as prudent as they were enlightened, they deemed it necessary to keep these things under the veil of secrecy until it "pleased God to reveal them Himself."[4]

---

[4] They also judged it best to say nothing of this to Cardinal Billiet, the Archbishop of Chambéry (in light of his old age of 85 years), His Eminence being very upset at the time by false revelations that were troubling a diocese in Savoy.

That was why the Community would remain unaware of the signal graces with which it was being favored in one of its members—the one who was, humanly speaking, the least fit to receive them.

That was also why, regarding the spiritual directors' advice as sacred instructions, our Very Honorable Mother Thérèse-Eugénie Revel never omitted to write down, with a scrupulous exactitude, the communications of the humble Lay Sister, whom, moreover, Our Lord had ordered to keep nothing hidden from her Superiors: "Tell your Mothers to write down everything, what comes from Me and even what comes from you. There is no harm in your defects being seen. I desire that you show everything that happens within you for the good that it is to do later when you are in Heaven.

"You must not lose courage. This work is long, but it pleases Me much."

A striking detail. Sister Mary Martha could not check her Superior's work. But Our Lord checked. Sometimes out of forgetfulness or a lack of time, our Very Honorable Mother would omit certain words. What a surprise when the following day our Sister would return with this statement from Jesus: "Your Mother did not write down these words. I want them written down."

With such instructions confirming those of the spiritual directors, we can imagine the religious care taken by our Very Honorable Mother and the Directress to not lose anything transmitted to them by their daughter.[5] This can be seen by the

---

[5] Sister Mary Martha's directress, our Very Honorable Sister Marie-Alexis Blanc, contributed half of the information compiled. We found notes written in her hand and copied verbatim by our Very Honorable Mother Thérèse-Eugénie.

following declaration placed at the beginning of the manuscripts: "We place here in the presence of God and of our Holy Founders, out of obedience and in the most exact manner possible, what we believe to be sent us from Heaven through an all-loving predilection of the Divine Heart of Jesus, for the happiness of our Community and for the good of souls."

\*\*\*

Guided by the notes of the Confidantes, we shall continue to affectionately follow our Sister.

One should not expect to encounter thunder and lightning. If a cloistered religious sanctifies herself, it is not through the greatness and variety of the works, but rather through the intensity and purity of the love she brings to the simplest things.

And when this religious is a Visitandine, there is not even a place in the Rule for great austerities. We know that St. Francis de Sales, in founding the Order of the Visitation, was devising a new concept: he was creating—in order to make it accessible to those of average health—a type of life where the spirit of interior sacrifice, of death to self, would compensate in the eyes of God for what, until then, had been considered one of the constituent elements of all religious life, and would have as much benefit, if not more, for individual sanctification as exterior austerities.

If, from the point of view of austerities, Sister Mary Martha was among the exceptions willed by God and foreseen by the Holy Founders, with allowances being made for "supernatural" conditions that would remain the secret of the Superiors, one can certainly say that her virtues and outward life did not remove her from the humble Visitandine path. When viewed from the outside, no religious life presents more humdrum uniformity than her own. From the time of her novitiate, the Superiors entrusted her with the job of boarding school refectorian. She maintained this position until her final days. There she spent her life, in self-effacement, in the monotony of occupations that were always the same, far from excitement, often even far from the company of her Sisters… but not in idleness! Considerable, in fact, was the daily labor of our dear Sister.

In addition to everything pertaining to the painstaking and demanding operation of the refectory, there was also the upkeep of the choir and of several rooms of the boarding school and their adjoining areas.

Let us add the harvesting of fruit, with which she was continuously tasked and which at times required her to be at work prior to four o'clock in the morning…

The totality of work left her hardly any other respite than the time for prayer.

But beneath the veil of uniformly repeated occupations having no interest to the human eye, what an intense interior life and what heavenly illuminations! Our Lord seems to have drawn her to Himself from a very early age, having entrusted her with a kind of personal "mission," having unceasingly excited her to piety, formed her in virtue and supported her in her "task." That is what these pages, from this point forward, are going to try to relive.

In following our Sister in the great contours of her physiognomy or in the smaller features, one will have the impression of a perfect unity. Three words sum up her interior life: Manger, Tabernacle, and Calvary. Three words designating allurements that are wondrously harmonized and united: the Child Jesus, the Eucharistic Jesus, and the Crucified Jesus. But it is always the same Lord Jesus drawing this soul, making Himself both Master and Model, and, as a benevolent "Catechist," adapting Himself to the littleness of His pupil. The beauty of this life, its distinctive character and, let us add, its beneficent charm, especially consisted in this: the direct, constant, and loving action of Jesus.

Our Lord asked much from Sister Mary Martha. But He was proportionately generous. She had nothing; He gave. She knew nothing; He instructed. She could do nothing; He raised up, led, and sustained.

# CHAPTER 6

# THE CHOSEN ONE OF JESUS CRUCIFIED

IN the month of September 1867, the cholera had swept down on our land of Savoy, claiming everywhere, but especially in the city of Chambéry, very numerous casualties.

It was at this time, in order to welcome the poor little orphans left by the epidemic, that Canon Costa de Beauregard—this big-hearted priest whom the public regards as a saint and whose cause is being introduced—founded Le Bocage Orphanage.[1]

At the Visitation, it was not without apprehension that we anticipated the day set for the students' return. Our Mothers charged Sister Mary Martha with the task of praying to the Divine Redeemer to preserve the Community. Jesus, inclining towards the docile mediatrix, confided her this benevolent response: "Fear nothing. You are in the monastery as in the ark of Noah. The plague will come to the door, but it shall not penetrate inside. As for the students, you must not delay their return. They will not bring the plague and, once inside the House, they shall be protected."

In fact, the Superior noted that many students came that year, and that we had no problems.

---

[1] This admirable work is currently [in 1928] directed by Fr. Ernest Costa de Beauregard, nephew of the founder. (See the very interesting biography *Une âme de Saint: le Chanoine Camille Costa de Beauregard*, by Ernest Costa de Beauregard, p. 64.)

In giving these assurances, Our Lord requested certain penitential practices and, in particular, prayers in honor of the Holy Wounds.

For some time, in fact, the Divine Savior had called Sister Mary Martha to the magnificent task of offering up the merits of His Passion: "He urged her to offer up at each moment His Holy Wounds to God the Father for the needs of Holy Church and of the Community, for the conversion of sinners, and principally for the souls in Purgatory" (Manuscript).

"With My Holy Wounds," Jesus said, "you have all the riches of Heaven to rain down upon the earth.

"You must offer up the wealth of My Holy Wounds. You must not remain poor, for your Father is truly rich. Your riches—they are My Holy Passion.

"Something pains me," He added, "it is that there are souls who regard devotion to My Wounds as strange, as contemptible, as something inappropriate… that is why it falls and is forgotten.

"In Heaven, I have Saints who had a great devotion to My Holy Wounds, but on earth there is almost no one who honors Me in this way."

This complaint is only too well-founded! In a world where "enjoyment" appears to be the only preoccupation, how many people, Christians even, have lost the sense of sacrifice! Too few souls understand the Cross! Too few endeavor to meditate on the Passion of Our Lord Jesus Christ, what St. Francis de Sales so rightly calls "the true school of love, the sweetest and most violent incentive to piety."[2]

---

[2] *Treatise on the Love of God*, bk. 12, chap. 13.

Now Jesus does not want this inexhaustible mine to stay unexploited, that the fruits of His sufferings should remain forgotten and lost.

To accomplish His designs of love on the world, He chose— Is this not His custom?—the humblest of instruments.

From the end of 1866, this great devotion of Sister Mary Martha's had become apparent. In September 1867, during a Triduum of graces, the "mission" that was to imprint such a distinctive character on her life, and which she gladly called her "task," appeared more clearly to her.

On the twenty-fifth of that month, as our Sister was feeling very unwell at the morning Obedience,[3] the Superior ordered her to go to bed. She had hardly done so when the voice of Our Lord made itself heard in her soul: "I want you to observe three days here in honor of the three Divine Persons."

And this was, for the dear Seer, three days of exceptional graces. All the splendor of Heaven came to illuminate the narrow cell, upon which the Holy Trinity descended.

**The Glory.** – On the twenty-sixth, at the time of the *Sanctus* of the Mass, Sister Mary Martha went into ecstasy. God the Father presented Himself to her gaze above a magnificent altar and, showing her Jesus, said to her, "I give you Him Whom you offer to Me so often. I associate you with my Angels. Know that you have more power than they, for you can unceasingly offer Me the Wounds of My Divine Son for sinners and they can only contemplate them."

The Seraphim surrounded their Creator. The angelic host appeared exclusively occupied in serving God. She saw all of

---

[3] The "morning" Obedience was held around noon. See also chap. 4, n. 1.

the Saints prostrate in profound adoration… whilst she tasted a little of "what the eye of man has not seen, what the ear has not heard, and what the human mind cannot understand." Our Sister did not find the words to explain this.

**The Manger.** – On the second day, Sister Mary Martha was transported in spirit to the interior of Bethlehem's stable. The Child Jesus appeared to her lying in the manger, with St. Joseph and the angels contemplating Him in silent adoration.

The Most Blessed Virgin took Him and placed Him in her arms, saying, "My daughter, I give Him to you as I gave Him to the world."

Her soul then received vivid lights about the ravishing mystery of the Nativity, about the poverty of Our Lord, the model of religious souls, about the self-divesting God requires of His Spouses; about the generosity He demands of them to advance on this path of poverty and renunciation: "They must be naked, completely naked. The religious life is not a life of enjoyment; it is all poverty, obedience, and suffering."

At that moment, the manuscripts state, in words we shall quote verbatim, two paths appeared before our Sister's eyes.

"The first is that of the soul who abandons itself to Our Lord's will. Love has crucified it, and after having traveled the same path as Jesus, it goes straight to Heaven. The second one is that of souls who travel out of compulsion. They perform their actions because they have to do them… It is not love that drives them. They have much trouble and hardly advance.

"To enter the first path, two things are necessary: first, the opening up of the heart and simple obedience; secondly, fidelity in not resisting any lights from one's conscience.

"My daughter, ask of Me this grace for all religious souls."

**The Cross.** – On the third day, Sister Mary Martha then saw, in a new rapture, the Heavenly Court surrounding the three Divine Persons.

God the Father, drawing from Himself His Spirit like a ray of fire, imparted it to her soul. "Herein," He declared, "are light, suffering, and love!… The love shall be for Me, the light for discovering My will, the suffering for suffering from moment to moment…"

Then, inviting her to contemplate the Cross of His Son, the Heavenly Father gave her to better understand the Wounds of Jesus for her personal good. At the same time, in a ray of light that shot out from earth to Heaven, she clearly saw her "mission" and how she was to offer up the merits of Jesus's Wounds for the entire world.

God the Father also gave her to understand the significance of these visions. The last two, which were figures of the hidden life and the crucified life, were in order to show her the path to the first: eternal glory.

One can easily understand how, at the end of these three days, the dear Seer, illuminated by divine lights, could only with difficulty open her eyes to the sight of earthly and sensible things. Her soul remained immersed in an interior contemplation which nothing could distract! In the words of our Very Honorable Mother, "she had only her body on the earth."

Three days later, on October 2, Sister Mary Martha was present at a "taking of the habit" when, the vault of Heaven opening, she saw the same ceremony unfold in a quite otherworldly splendor. All of the Visitation in Heaven were present to welcome the young novice, prophesying that she would become a fervent religious.[4] St. Modesta[5] was there as well, very pleased to have the new fiancée as her protégée.[6]

Our first Mothers, addressing themselves to Sister Mary Martha, said to her joyfully, "The Eternal Father has given our Holy Order His Son in three manners: firstly, Jesus Christ Crucified, the Cross, His Holy Wounds, to this House more particularly; secondly, His Sacred Heart; and thirdly, the Child Jesus."

These are family possessions. In going back to the origins of the Institute, we find in the life of Mother Anne-Marguerite Clément,[7] a contemporary of St. Jane de Chantal, these three devotions, which marked all Religious formed by her.

Perhaps this soul, as we would like to believe, was equally privileged, who, together with our Holy Mother Foundress, came to recall these things to the chosen one of God, especially emphasizing the Passion and Wounds of the Savior.

On the following October 23, the Very Honorable Mother Marie-Pauline Deglapigny insisted on this same point. Appearing to her former daughter, she confirmed to her this gift of the Holy Wounds: "The Visitation always had great riches, but they were not complete. Therefore, blessed was the day I left the earth, because instead of having only the Heart of Our Lord to honor, you will have (as a sensible object of your devotion)

---

[4] This was our dear Sister Marie-Modeste d'Agoûlt.

[5] Virgin and martyr, whose holy body rests in a reliquary beneath the main altar of the Visitation church.

[6] Modeste, already identified in note 4 above as the name taken by the novice, is the French equivalent of the name Modesta.—Trans.

[7] See Auguste Saudreau, *Les tendresses du Seigneur pour une âme fidèle, ou Vie de la Mère Anne-Marguerite Clément, première supérieure des monastères de la Visitation de Montargis et de Melun, 1593-1661* (Paris: Charles Amat, 1915).

all of His Holy Humanity, that is to say His Sacred Wounds. I have asked for this grace."

St. Francis de Sales, our blessed Father, who very often visited his dear daughter to paternally instruct her, did not fail to confirm her in the certitude of her mission: "God has chosen you to complete the devotion to the Sacred Heart; the Heart was shown to Blessed Margaret Mary and the Holy Wounds to my little Mary Martha!... It is a joy for my paternal heart that this honor be rendered by you to Jesus Crucified!"

The Most Blessed Virgin also came on one feast of the Visitation to confirm the young Sister in her path. Accompanied by the Holy Founders and St. Margaret Mary, she said with kindness, "I give my Fruit to the Visitation as I carried Him to my cousin Elizabeth. Your Holy Founder reproduced the works, meekness, and humility of my Son; Holy Mother de Chantal, my generosity, in overcoming all obstacles to unite herself to Jesus and to doing His Holy Will; your Blessed Sister Margaret Mary reproduced the Sacred Heart of my Son to give it to the world... And you, my daughter, you are chosen to hold back the Justice of God, by offering up the merits of the Passion and Holy Wounds of my only beloved Son Jesus."

But from Our Lord especially His humble Servant received, multiple times, the assurance that she was truly called to revive devotion to the redeeming Wounds: "I have chosen you to reawaken devotion to My Holy Passion in the unfortunate time in which you are living." Then, showing her His Holy Wounds as a book He wanted to teach her to read, the good Master added, "Do not move your eyes from this book and you will learn from it more than the greatest scholars. Prayer to the Holy Wounds encompasses everything."

He asked her to unceasingly offer His Divine Wounds for the salvation of the world: "My daughter, the world will be more or less troubled according to whether you accomplish your task. You are chosen to satisfy My justice.

"I desire, through this devotion, that not only the souls with whom you live be made holy, but many others still.

"I have chosen you to offer up the merits of My Holy Passion for all; but I desire that you still be hidden. It is for Me to make known later that it is by this means that the world shall be saved—and also by the hands of My Immaculate Mother."

To stir up Sister Mary Martha's zeal, Our Lord was pleased to disclose to her the benefits of this devotion, the inestimable treasures of these founts of life.

"My daughter, each time that you offer My Father the merits of My Divine Wounds, you gain an immense fortune.

"My Father delights in the offering of My Sacred Wounds and of My Holy Mother's sorrows. To offer Him My Wounds is to offer Him His glory, it is to offer Heaven to Heaven.

"One of my creatures betrayed Me and sold My blood; but you can so easily repurchase it drop by drop!... A single drop suffices to purify the earth and you do not think of it! You do not know its value!"

Showing His Beloved these "fountains of salvation" as suspended between Heaven and earth, He said: "My daughter, recognize the treasure of the world... The world does not want to recognize it..."

Jesus urged her—and urges us along with her—to come with confidence to this treasure: "He who is in need, let him come with faith and confidence, let him continuously draw from the treasure of My Passion.

"Behold what pays for all those who have debts.

"One must not fear showing My Wounds to souls. The way of My Wounds is so simple and so easy for getting to Heaven.

"In the contemplation of My Wounds, one finds everything for oneself and for others."

Jesus redoubled the encouraging promises:

"I will grant everything asked of Me through devotion to the Holy Wounds. Those who honor them shall have a true knowledge of Jesus Christ.

"My daughter, where were the Saints made, if not in My Wounds? From My Wounds come fruits of holiness. Just as gold that is purified in the crucible becomes more beautiful, in the same way you must put your soul and those of your Sisters in My Sacred Wounds—there they shall be perfected like gold in the furnace."

The Holy Wounds have a wondrous efficacy in converting sinners.

One day, Sister Mary Martha, seized with anguish at the thought of the earth's crimes, exclaimed, "My Jesus, take care of your children, do not look at their sins."

The Divine Master, answering her appeal, taught her the following aspiration: "My Jesus, pardon and mercy through the merits of Thy Holy Wounds." Then he added, "Many people will experience the efficacy of this invocation."

"I desire," He stated another time, "that Priests often give it to their penitents in the Holy Tribunal.

"The sinner who says the following prayer will obtain conversion: 'Eternal Father, I offer Thee the Wounds of Our Lord Jesus Christ to heal the wounds of our souls.'"

The Holy Wounds are a balm and a consolation in suffering: "This aspiration must be repeated often with those who are ill: 'My Jesus, pardon and mercy through the merits of Thy Holy Wounds.' This prayer will relieve soul and body."

The Holy Wounds ensure a good death: "There will be no death for the soul who expires in My Wounds, they give true life."

# CHAPTER 7

## THE SHOWING OF THE HOLY WOUNDS

AND now, the object of this devotion will appear to us in a more concrete manner.

Jesus shows His Wounds, renewing appeals which—through His Confidante—are addressed to all souls. How life-giving to place oneself, with her, in the radiance of the redeeming Wounds! How profitable to listen to the appeals of the Savior!

\*\*\*

"After My Holy Mother," He said to Sister Mary Martha, "no soul has had like you the grace to contemplate day and night My Holy Wounds."

We read, in fact, from the pen of our Very Honorable Mother: "Our Lord shows her His Divine Wounds each day. They appear in a sensible manner to the eyes of her soul, sometimes radiant, which fills her with joy, and sometimes bloody, which induces in her an inexplicable martyrdom: 'I want you to see them thus, so that you better understand what I did in coming to earth to suffer for you.'"

In this wondrous display, the Savior at times presented Himself to His spouse with the totality of His adorable Wounds. Showing her His flesh torn in shreds, He said to her, "Wherever you find the Wounds of your Spouse, you must draw therefrom for the world—this is your work.

"Behold what I show to all souls, but only a few look at them. You, My daughter, take in everything from My Crown of Thorns to My Feet and contemplate."

Sometimes He showed her one only, apart from the others. And so it was one day He revealed to her His Right Foot, saying, "How much you must respect this Wound and hide yourself therein like the dove!"

Another time, it was His Left Hand: "My daughter, take from My Left Hand My merits for souls, so that they will be at My right for Eternity…";

His two adorable Feet: "Lead all of my creatures here… These openings are large enough to enclose all… The Wounds of My Sacred Feet are an ocean."[1]

His Head crowned with thorns: "My daughter, here you will take submission of judgment."

The Wound of His Divine Side: "Here you must take meekness and humility."

Consolation and intense love penetrated the soul of our Sister. She could not take her eyes away from the Holy Wounds, and our sweet Savior took pleasure in seeing her in speechless ecstasy: "My daughter, in contemplating them, you console Me… and in turn, I will console you with the vision of My glory for Eternity."

---

[1] Our ignorant Lay Sister subsequently asked her Superior, "Mother, what is an ocean?"

### The Crown of Thorns and the Wounds of the Head

A historian of St. Jane de Chantal,[2] describing the rule of life she had adopted from the time of her entry into religious life, tells us that each evening she would retire "into one of Our Lord's Wounds," and that, on Fridays, she chose "the scars of His adorable Head."

It seems good for us to recall here the devotion of our Holy Foundress to the Wounded Head of Jesus. For of Sister Mary Martha also, the Divine Master asked a very special cult of veneration, reparation, and love for His august, thorn-crowned Head.

The Crown of Thorns was for Him a cause of particularly cruel sufferings. "My Crown of Thorns caused me more suffering than all My other Wounds,"[3] He confided to His spouse. "It was My most cruel suffering after the Garden of Olives. To alleviate it, you must observe your Rule well."

It is, for the soul faithful to its imitation, a source of merits. "Behold," He said, "this Head which was pierced for love of you, and by whose merits you must one day be crowned. It is the Crown of Thorns that will merit you the crown of glory."

It is the gift of choice that Our Lord gives to His friends: "My Crown of Thorns, I give it to My privileged ones. It is the special possession of My spouses. It is the glory of the Blessed, but for my beloved on earth, it is a suffering." (From the place of each

---

[2] Henry de Maupas du Tour, *La Vie de la Vénérable Mère Jeanne Françoise Fremiot*, 8th ed. (Paris: Siméon Piget, 1667), 115.

[3] The careful examination of the wounds on the nape of the neck (as they appear on the Holy Shroud of Turin) makes us understand the revelation of Our Lord to the little Lay Sister of the Visitation in Chambéry, Sister Mary Martha Chambon: "My crown of thorns caused Me more suffering than all My other wounds" (*Bulletin du Saint Suaire*, June 1925, p. 14).

thorn, our Sister saw shoot forth a ray of glory impossible to describe.) "My true servants try to suffer as I; but no one can attain the degree of suffering that I endured."

From these souls, Jesus seeks a more tender compassion for His adorable Head. Let us hear this cry of the heart that He addresses to Sister Mary Martha in revealing to her His bloody Head, all pierced and revealing so much suffering that the poor little one would not know with what words to express it. "Behold the One Whom you seek! See what a state He is in!… Look… extract these thorns from My Head by offering to My Father the merits of My Wounds for sinners… Go in search of souls!"

We see in these appeals of the Savior, ever repeating like an echo of the eternal "I thirst," the preoccupation with saving souls: "Go in search of souls!"

A striking contrast: Then Jesus presented Himself to the overjoyed eyes of our young Sister with this same Crown, all radiant with a brilliant glory: "My Crown of Thorns shall illuminate Heaven and all the Blessed!"

Joy of the just, the Holy Crown is, on the other hand, an object of terror for the wicked. This is what Sister Mary Martha perceived one day in a scene given her to contemplate by the One Who loved to instruct her by revealing to her the mysteries of the Beyond.

All illuminated with the splendors of this Divine Crown, the Judgment Seat where souls are judged appeared. Souls continuously passed before the Sovereign Judge. The souls who had been faithful during their life threw themselves with confidence into the arms of the Savior. The others, at the sight of the Holy Crown, and at the remembrance of the love of Our Lord that they had scorned, hurled themselves, in terror, into the eternal abyss.

So upsetting was this vision that the poor child was still trembling with fear and terror when she recounted it.

### The Wound of the Heart

If the Savior revealed all the beauty and all the riches of His Divine Wounds to the humble Lay Sister in this manner, with what tenderness did He open to her the treasures of His great wound of love!

But here, more than anywhere else, love directs the complaint. The invitation to love puts in the background the invitation to suffer. It is true that the one calls for the other: does not true love blossom in sacrifice and in reparation?

"Behold the Fount from which you must draw everything," Jesus said to Sister Mary Martha, showing her His Wounds in a luminous splendor and that of His Sacred Heart shining amongst the others with an incomparable brilliance: "Come here into the Wound of My Divine Side… This is the Wound of Love from which shoot forth living flames!"

At the same time, He made known His immense desire to see diffused the graces with which His Heart overflows: "Place your lips here to draw charity and to spread it out throughout the world. Place here your hand to take My treasures… I can no longer contain them, so much do I desire to give them.

"Come receive the effusion of My Heart, which desires to pour out its overflow. I wish to pour into you from My abundance…"

But first, Jesus calls for union with His Heart, which is a prerequisite for any apostolate. He does this at each moment, in diverse manners, with overtones that stir up souls, confound timidity, and condemn coldness.

On one feast day of the Sacred Heart, revealing to His chosen one this "Wound of Love," which was wide open, He told her: "This is where you are... this is where I place you!"

"This is your center. No one can prevent you from loving it or make you love it without your heart's consent. Everything creatures will say cannot take away from you your treasure, your love! I want you to love Me without human support."

On another day: "Do as the butterfly—fly here into My Heart! When a soul is deeply immersed within the Wound that it honors, it remains there."

"Oh, my Jesus, could You have given me a place that suits me better!"

Let us listen still: "If you wish to enter into the light of the Lord, you must penetrate into My Divine Heart... If you wish to know the depths of mercy of Him Who loves you so much, you must 'connect' to the opening of My Sacred Heart with respect and humility.

"I desire that all hearts enter into Mine. It is there that your Father St. Francis drew his maxims. It is in My Heart that one finds peace."

This Sacred Heart, open to the faithful as a refuge, also desires to find in our hearts a refuge and a place of repose. Let us hear these appeals addressed to Sister Mary Martha:

"Do you love me?"

"Yes, good Master, I do love you!"

"Very well then, the brides must not leave their Bridegroom all alone... O My bride, My Heart no longer knows where to go to rest... I have chosen for Myself a victim in whose heart I wish to take My repose—what ingratitude if you should push Me away!"

"Yes, my Jesus, since You desire to come and take Your repose in me, purify me… I shall be as the dove—I shall hide in Your openings."

"Yes, My daughter, be as the dove, enter into My Heart… Come and take for yourself and for souls. Expand in My Heart for all those who do not do so."

And this love of our poor hearts, Jesus values it so much that He goes so far as to beg for it.

Appearing one day in all the beauty of His Resurrection, He said to His beloved, "Behold, My daughter, how I beg like a poor man! I call My children one by one… I wait for them." Then taking the actual appearance of a beggar, He repeated, full of sadness at seeing His loving gestures ignored, "I beg for perfect love, but most, even among the souls of religious, refuse Me this love!… My daughter, love Me, above all else, for My sake."

Referring to our Sister St. Margaret Mary, whose gaze "devoured" the Heart of Jesus, He said to her, "This one loved Me with this pure love, for Me alone."

And Sister Mary Martha tried to love with this same love. Like an immense fire, the Sacred Heart drew her to Himself by its indescribable heat… She went towards her Beloved in rushes of love that consumed her, but which, at the same time, left in her soul an all-divine sweetness.

"If you saw how fully you possess My Heart," the good Master said, "the sight would astound you! You are the beloved of My Heart. From now on, you shall neither love nor breathe except by My Heart."

# CHAPTER 8

## SISTER MARY MARTHA'S
## RESPONSE TO JESUS'S DESIRES

OVED within the deepest recesses of her being, our dear Sister allowed herself to be penetrated with an ever-growing love for the adorable Wounds of the Savior.

"Love has such power," St. Francis de Sales says, "that it draws to itself the qualities of the object loved." With Sister Mary Martha, the transformation produced by this gaze of sorrowful attentiveness was so profound that she at times believed herself to be one with the suffering Jesus and that the Wounds of her Spouse had become her own.

Her most ardent desire was to ignite the world with the sentiments of love and gratitude that these Wounds ought to inspire, ready to give her own life to propagate a devotion she wanted to be immense, impassioned, and limitless.

Personally, our Sister had responded to the call from the Divine Master in a positive and official manner.

On October 17, 1867, our Very Honorable Mother Thérèse-Eugénie, wrote up, in fact, in the name of her dear child, the following pact:

"I, Sister Mary Martha Chambon, promise Our Lord Jesus Christ to offer myself each morning to God the Father, in union with the Divine Wounds of Jesus Crucified, for the salvation of the entire world and for the good and perfection of my Community.

"I shall adore Him in all hearts who receive Him in the Holy Eucharist... I shall thank Him for coming into so many hearts who are so little prepared.

"I promise Our Lord to offer every ten minutes—with the help of His grace and in a spirit of obedience—the Divine Wounds of His Sacred Body to the Eternal Father... to unite all my actions to His Holy Wounds, according to the intentions of His Adorable Heart, for the triumph of Holy Church, for sinners and the souls in Purgatory, for all the needs of my Community, those of the Novitiate and of the Boarding School, and in atonement for all the offenses committed therein. All of this through love, without the obligation of sin" (in case of forgetfulness).

The invocation for this offering was the following: "Eternal Father, I offer Thee the Wounds of Our Lord Jesus Christ to heal the wounds of our souls."

Sister Mary Martha had promised to recite this invocation "every ten minutes," but there hardly passed a moment in the day when her mouth did not renew it, joining to it this second invocation: "My Jesus, pardon and mercy through the merits of Thy Holy Wounds."

The life of our dear Sister thus became simultaneously a continuous immolation and an uninterrupted prayer—union with God and a profound recollection could be seen in her physiognomy. In seeing her, one was struck by her almost always closed eyes and her lips unceasingly whispering a prayer.

If, moreover, her ardor decreased, if the precious offering rose less often from her heart to Heaven, Jesus would not delay in presenting Himself to her in the pitiable state to which our iniquities reduced Him and, showing His Wounds, making these loving reproaches: "They are always watching you, even when you forget, you who ought to be looking at them always… They are all fresh, you must offer them as if for the first time… I have already shown them to you so often that it ought to be enough; but no, I must always reawaken your fervor."

It was with three strands of large thorns in His Crown that the Savior came one day to rouse His spouse's keen compassion. The spectacle was so sorrowful and moving that Sister Mary Martha could not help crying out, "O my Jesus, give me then a participation in this frightful torment!"

Her prayer was immediately answered. Head pains of extraordinary violence seized her to the point that she could no longer hold herself up.

Presenting Himself to her as in a picture, "You must copy Me," He implored her one day, in a tone of indescribable gentleness and ardent desire. "You must copy me!… Painters make pictures that conform little to the original; but in this case, it is I Who am the painter and Who make My image in you if you look at Me."

Our Sister lent herself with docility to the activity of the Master, for some time afterward He asked her, "My daughter, do you want to be crucified, or do you want to be glorified?"

"Good Master, I prefer to be crucified."

It was especially at the time of her annual retreats that our fervent Sister received, with marks of tenderness from her Divine Spouse, more urgent appeals to devotion to the Holy Wounds and to the Crucifixion. As she applied herself to her "task," Our Lord's activity continued, sweetly but irresistibly.

From the retreat of 1867, we note this invitation, as beautiful as it is striking: "I would like to see all of My brides become crucifixes!"

The following year, on the first day of her solitude,[1] Sister Mary Martha heard the Eucharistic Jesus tell her these loving words: "I give Myself to you to make your retreat. Retire into your heart and close the door so we can be 'one-to-one.' This is Heaven."

Then presenting the image of the Crucifix to her gaze: "Do you see in your heart the beautiful body of the little Child Jesus, how it has become... You must recount in your soul the torn state in which you see Me."

In the evening, as our Sister was lying on the floor of her cell for the night, her Divine Priest made her to hear these words: "Say to Me now: Jesus, behold Your victim."

Her soul initially shuddered and resisted this vision of suffering. Her nature was revolted at the cross that had been offered her. There was a terrible struggle until midnight. But then Jesus appeared to His Servant, His Forehead torn and bloody, all of His Body broken, and His Face soiled, bruised, and furrowed with tears. "My daughter," He said to her, "for your retreat book, your Superior gave you the Crucifix... here it is!"

After several hours of silent contemplation, Our Lord made her to feel the pain of two Wounds that bloodied the top of His Head and the pain He had sustained in His most august Face when the executioners struck Him a heavy blow. The very painful sensation of these three injuries stayed with her the entire night. "You are a martyr of Jesus Christ," declared Jesus the

---

[1] A retreat of eight or ten days that each religious makes individually.

Savior, "prepare yourself to receive all of My Wounds, one after the other. You will be a martyr who goes on living."

From time to time, our adorable Master rewarded the efforts and zeal of His humble spouse with truly divine tenderness.

In September 1867, like the Virgin of Sorrows, Sister Mary Martha had the distinct privilege of receiving in her arms the Most Sacred Body of Jesus Christ. At the same time, she received this lesson: "To contemplate the Wounds of Jesus well, you must not have any attachment in your heart, not even to the slightest voluntary imperfection."

Our Sister kept this precious deposit from the end of Vespers until 5:45 p.m., that is to say for a duration of over two hours. She contemplated the adorable Wounds one by one, in the same order and with the same sentiments taught to her by the Mother of God, offering them without interruption to God the Father for the salvation of the world. "The Creator seemed so pleased," stated the blessed Privileged One, "to receive His Divine Son from such miserable hands!"

Another time, during the retreat of September 1881, she found herself in a very difficult interior state: her heart remained dry and her prayer without unction. "My sweet Jesus," she said, "I want, despite everything, to do my duty, which is to offer unceasingly Your Divine Wounds."

Sister Mary Martha prayed thus for three quarters of an hour... Then, Jesus came to her: "My daughter, do you think I could remain deaf to souls who invoke My Holy Wounds? I do not have the ungrateful heart of the creature—I take account of everything! My Heart is large, My Heart is sensitive! The Wound of My Sacred Heart opens itself up wide to take in all of your needs!"

At that same moment, she saw the Wounds of the Savior as an equal number of suns whose brightness she could not withstand; the Crown of Thorns and the Heart especially appeared to her as centers of light. "My daughter, this is what is in store for you to see… After having invoked them well during your life, you shall contemplate them thus for Eternity."

"Oh, my Sister," the pious child said to our Very Honorable Sister and former Mother Thérèse-Eugénie, "it is so beautiful that one cannot describe it—gold and precious stones are nothing in comparison!"

# CHAPTER 9

## THE STIGMATA & LIVING ONLY ON HOLY COMMUNION

**S**HOULD it be surprising that the Divine Master wanted to imprint the external signs of crucified love on this victim, who was chosen for a redemptive mission and associated in a special way with the work of Our Lord Jesus Christ?

"You are a martyr of Jesus Christ," He declared to her one day. "Prepare yourself to receive all of My Wounds, one after the other."

On June 12, 1874, at daybreak on the feast of the Sacred Heart, Sister Mary Martha was lying on the ground. As she was offering herself to God the Father in so intimate a union with His Divine Son that it seemed to her she had been subsumed into Him, Our Lord Jesus Christ appeared to her. She immediately experienced the sensation of a burning sword piercing her left foot.

Our two former Mothers Marie-Alexis Blanc and Thérèse-Eugénie Revel examined the wound. It was quite deep, as wide as a fifty-centime coin, and very painful.

Fifteen days later, the Chosen One of Christ received the same wound on her right foot. So strong, this time, was the pain, that Sister Mary Martha could barely walk.

"A mortifying anxiety came over the poor child, who dreaded that the new favor bestowed upon her would be discovered in the Community. She beseeched Jesus to withdraw it from her or to at least make it completely internal. For several months she was unable to obtain this.

"Every Wednesday, blood began to flow from these wounds, and would not stop until Friday evenings. The first times, the blood was so abundant that her shoe was completely filled with it" (Deposition of our Very Honorable Mother Thérèse-Eugénie).

In the month of November, Jesus, finally yielding to His Spouse's entreaties, no longer left anything of these wounds except for a small opening that lightly oozed on Fridays.

In May of the following year, the stigmata became more active again, bleeding abundantly three times per week. However, by means of new and more fervent supplications, Sister Mary Martha obtained from the Savior that He transform this suffering into one less apparent (in August 1875).

The wounds closed. Even the scars disappeared. The blood rushed violently to her head, where she suffered cruel pains. These physical sufferings, however, were nothing compared to the spiritual torments to which she was subjected. She therefore experienced the truth of the words spoken to her one day by our Sister St. Margaret Mary: "Having Jesus Crucified in one's heart is an even greater grace than the stigmata; it is more hidden."

And so, in this form, Sister Mary Martha was stigmatized like few souls will ever be!

\*\*\*

By another means, no less effective, the Divine Master, in this same period, strengthened his hold on the soul of His Bride.

As if to show her that He was to suffice for her in everything, He wanted, for a period of more than four years, for her to have no other food than the Holy Eucharist.

It was little by little, however, that He led her to this extraordinary state.

One can follow our Sister almost day by day throughout the months of preparation. We shall limit ourselves to the final notes recorded in the manuscripts:

"On January 25, 1869, she took nothing, not even a drop of water. On the twenty-sixth and twenty-seventh, consumed with thirst, she quenched herself with a little bit of cold water. On the twenty-eighth, in the afternoon, we brought her a small cup of water with sugar which immediately caused her great stomach pains.

"On the following days, she took only water, with the exception of one day when she obtained Our Lord's permission to go to the refectory to calm the neighbor who was worried about her.

"On Shrove Tuesday, February 9, 1869, she went with everyone to the community room to participate in recreation and drank a coffee with milk. She then took nothing until the first Sunday of Lent when she had some broth that made her ill.

"We could not help ourselves at the beginning of Lent from bringing her, out of compassion, two fingers of sweet wine or some other comfort, once or twice a week; but it was necessary for her to renounce it. The dear child had to content herself a day here and there with a few drops of cold water. Soon the Absolute Master of souls and bodies withdrew from her even this slight relief."

From that point forward, it would be four and a half years that Holy Communion was absolutely her only food. "However, our little Sister," the Superior wrote, "enjoyed robust health. She was even doing better than when she took her meals like everyone else. She washes and scrubs the floors, it is a marvel! At the account rendering, she joyfully assures us: 'I don't feel weak at all; I did my work today with such ease!... I even have more strength than usual.'"

And despite the day's hard work, she was seen sacrificing her sleep in the silence of the nights at the feet of Jesus in the Most Blessed Sacrament.

As the manuscript notes, however, Sister Mary Martha did sometimes feel her strength fail. Our Lord permitted it for the satisfaction He experienced in seeing her run to Him in all the simplicity of her soul, in seeing her prostrate before the choir grill, humbling herself, kissing the ground and lovingly complaining: "See, my Jesus, I have no more strength than this dust."

At the humility of such a prayer, Jesus knew not how to resist; He opened His Sacred Heart, all radiant with light: "Behold your strength... Come receive Me. I shall be like an oil that spreads throughout your members to strengthen you."

New blood then seemed to circulate in her veins, communicating to her a marvelous strength. She ran to her work and confronted its excesses without trouble, with the help of her Beloved.

Sometimes Jesus's victim experienced the "martyrdom of hunger." Her Divine Master judged well in His mysterious designs to let her endure these consuming torments, but while indicating to her the source of effective relief: "When you are hungry, pray by pressing your lips to My Heart."

Then, after she had suffered a long time, pleased with her soul's fidelity, He revealed His Wounds to her, "flooded" His little servant "with Himself," and drew her to His Heart: "Come, My Beloved, take your food from My Wounds!... Take... You shall eat well, you shall always be hungry, you shall never be satisfied.

"My daughter, be like a little bird—I feed it, no one prepares it anything. Come and 'peck' here inside; feed from My Wounds."

"It seems to her that she drinks abundantly from the Sacred Side of Jesus... All earthly joys are nothing in comparison to the joy that is hers in these moments. It is a joy that she does not experience when she wants... neither can she distract herself from it when God gives it to her... This joy follows her everywhere and her entire being is filled with it" (Manuscript).

However, it was a very great sorrow for Sister Mary Martha to feel herself outside of the communal life. She confided this to her Holy Founder: "Father, do not permit me to be lost by doing differently than what you have set forth."

This tender Father reassured her: "My daughter, follow well the path Jesus has set forth for you—this is your Rule."

Still not satisfied, she continued her complaints: "My God, I suffer so much in not going to the refectory with the others."

"Know, My daughter," the Savior answered, "that I have My times for giving My graces. When you went to the refectory, I gave them to you through fulfilling your Rule; now, it is in another manner. In a Community, one must follow one's path without looking at that of others."

Having lived in this truly miraculous way for over four years, Our Lord then allowed Sister Mary Martha to resume her ordinary meals little by little. She had been asking permission for this almost every day.

Finally yielding to her supplications at the end of September 1873, her Divine Master allowed her to return to the refectory.

"She had already been making this request for a few months," recounted the faithful narrator of her life, "and we had responded: 'We need proof that Jesus wants it. We are going to give you a little bit of food for eight days; if it doesn't make you ill, we will recognize it as God's Will.' But the simple little soup that she took made her suffer so horribly that we had to stop there... This time, on September 20, 1873, we began the test again to assure ourselves of God's Will: the food did not hurt her. After a trial of a few days, a place was set for her again at the refectory.

"She goes to all of the meals with a consolation like no other for being able to follow the Community in this."

But, from her "Eucharistic diet," she maintained a total detachment from all that was not God. She no longer belonged to herself. She belonged to Jesus. With Him, she belonged to souls. In their favor, she was fulfilling her "mission"…

# CHAPTER 10

## THE HOLY WOUNDS DEVOTION
## AND THE COMMUNITY

HE "mission" of Sister Mary Martha was, in the first place, to continuously offer up the merits of the Holy Wounds of Our Lord Jesus Christ for the needs of the Church militant, for the Church suffering, and, in a special way, for the Community. She was heroically faithful to this, as we have already stated. And we shall have the opportunity, in what follows, to explain this in greater detail.

As for igniting throughout the entire world a movement of souls around the Divine Wounds, these Founts of Salvation, this pertained to the future and could not be accomplished during the life of our Sister: the very moving appeals of Jesus and His merciful promises were not to be known until after the death of His Chosen One.

"Your path," Our Lord had told her when a young religious, "is to make Me known and loved, especially in the future... One day, I shall reveal all of these things, and one will clearly see the graces I am giving you, you who are so miserable.

"It will take a long time to establish this devotion," He added. "It is necessary to work for it courageously."

The veil of the future seemed to partially lift before the eyes of the humble Lay Sister.

One day in the year 1868, when before the Most Blessed Sacrament, she saw herself similar to a rich garment from which each could take pieces to use in their turn: "I did not understand what my Good Master meant by this," she later admitted to the Superior.

If our Sister was not destined to witness here below the magnificent blossoming of a devotion so dear to her soul, she at least had the joy to see it take its first step by firmly being established within the Community. It was only just. Here, the duty of gratitude obliges our hearts, filled with emotion, to loudly proclaim the ineffable tenderness of the Savior in her regard.

Without any merit on our part, His gaze of predilection had long fixed itself on the humble family for which He had reserved choice graces out of consideration for His privileged bride. He Himself revealed to His Confidante: "For a long time I have loved you with a love of predilection. I have designs on this Community of which you are not aware; I rule it as a Father."

The Superiors—at the time the only depositaries of these merciful designs—knew how to recognize the precious gift that had been so generously offered to us. They zealously strove to respond to the Divine Master's desires.

In exchange for exceptional graces, Jesus only asked two additional practices from the Community, of which we shall briefly speak: the Holy Hour and the Rosary of the Holy Wounds.[1]

---

[1] This requires an explanation: Our Lord had only explicitly asked for the invocations to the Holy Wounds. To facilitate their recitation, our Mothers set them to rosary beads. The Divine Master repeatedly expressed His satisfaction with this and asked for this pious practice to be maintained.

At the time of the 1867 cholera, Our Lord expressed the desire that on every Friday a Holy Hour be made by five Sisters, each one assigned to honor one of His Wounds.

"The Superior," this Good Master said, "will select the Sisters, assigning to each one the Wound she is to honor. My Divine Feet will count for one Wound; My Crown of Thorns will be the fifth.[2] Since what I am asking is in addition to the Rule, the Sisters chosen for this Holy Hour must make it in their cells."

The Most Blessed Virgin united her request to that of her Divine Son through these words, pierced with sorrowful regret: "There is no House on earth where the Holy Wounds of Jesus are honored in a special way on Friday evenings.[3] It is necessary during this hour to contemplate the holy openings and to immerse yourselves in them."

The desire of Jesus and Mary was fulfilled. For many years, after Matins, five of our Sisters had the good fortune to honor the Holy Wounds of our sweet Savior in this way.

Not being privy to the graces received, the Novitiate—of which Sister Mary Martha was still a part—saw itself called, like that of Paray, to the honor of offering Jesus the beginnings of a homage He had requested with so many pleas. Our Very Honorable Sister Marie-Alexis, the Directress, had her little flock draw from a set of holy cards she had made which depicted different Wounds of Our Lord. Several kept these cards until

---

[2] This manner of praying in no way pretends to change the traditional number or order of the five Wounds honored by the Church on the feast consecrated to this mystery long ago, but it adds to it the veneration of the Holy Crown of Thorns and of the injuries inflicted on the Sacred Head of Our Lord (Remark of His Excellency Bishop Castellan in the September 13, 1924 edition of Chambéry's *Semaine religieuse*).

[3] This pertains to the nighttime Holy Hour rather than the one made in several communities between three and four in the afternoon.

death and did not cease to honor the Wound that had been designated to them.

As for the blessed Privileged One, who was called day and night to contemplate the Wounds of the Redeemer, Mary taught her how she was to perform this devout exercise: "My daughter," she told her, "the first time that I contemplated the Wounds of my dear Son was when His Most Holy Body was placed in my arms. I meditated on His sufferings and sought to make them pass into my own heart… I looked at His Divine Feet, one after the other… From there, I went to His Heart, where I saw this great opening, the most profound for my maternal heart… I contemplated the left hand, then the right, and then the Crown of Thorns. All of these Wounds pierced my heart. This was my own Passion. Seven swords are in my heart, and it is through my heart that the Sacred Wounds of my Divine Son must be honored.

"Out of humility I began with the Sacred Feet of Jesus, and I desire that you follow the same order."

It was at about this same time (1868) that, in accordance with Our Lord's intentions, the Superiors established the daily recitation of the "Rosary of the Holy Wounds."[4]

---

[4] This is how we are accustomed to reciting this Rosary: At the beginning, before the decades, the beautiful prayer for which a priest in Rome was given the inspiration:

"O Jesus, Divine Redeemer, be merciful to us and to the whole world. – R. Amen.

"Mighty God, Holy God, Immortal God, have mercy on us and on the whole world. – R. Amen.

"Grace and mercy, my Jesus, during the present dangers; cover us with Thy Precious Blood. – R. Amen.

"Eternal Father, have mercy on us through the Blood of Thine only Son Jesus Christ; have mercy on us, we beseech Thee. – R. Amen. Amen. Amen."

It was not without difficulty that the Superiors were able to have this practice adopted. Just as in Paray, out of an extreme zeal for the Rule, there was more than one objection made. The origin of this new prayer, moreover, was suspected: it may have seemed strange to the older Sisters that the devotional inclinations of a simple little Novice Lay Sister had taken on the force of law within the Community.

Our Mothers, as well as the dear Privileged One, suffered much on this account.

But Our Lord encouraged them: "My daughter, God's graces are not given without there being difficulty in fulfilling My Will. The prophets of the Old Law were forced to state repeatedly what God wanted... For you also, My daughter, this will be your cross."

"My Wounds are yours... The more you encounter opposition and obstacles, the more My grace will abound."

God the Father, holding a key in His Hand, seemed to threaten with an air of severity: "If you do not do what I want, I shall close the Founts and give them to others."

The patient and humble steadfastness of our Mothers Thérèse-Eugénie and Marie-Alexis triumphed little by little over all the obstacles. Our Lord's support for them was evident: One Sister, whose high intelligence and sound judgment had given her authority in the monastery, was the one most strongly

---

On the small beads: "My Jesus, pardon and mercy. – R. Through the merits of Thy Holy Wounds."

On the large beads: "Eternal Father, I offer Thee the Wounds of Our Lord Jesus Christ. – R. To heal the wounds of our souls."

These last two invocations are those given by Our Lord Himself, and to which He attached such beautiful promises. They were printed in Grenoble by Fr. Ambroise, Capuchin, prior to 1880, and even translated into Italian.

opposed to the new devotion. However, she was approached by the humble Lay Sister who had been entrusted with a message from the Master. She listened to her reveal something absolutely secret that had passed between her and Him in the depths of her soul, something she had never confided to anyone and which, consequently, Sister Mary Martha could not have known by any ordinary means. Surprised and converted, the Sister loyally allied herself with the cause and wanted to repair her past opposition by making small images of the Holy Wounds in order to propagate their veneration.

In light of this progress, the devil's fury was unable to contain itself. He especially went after our Sister, whom he ridiculed as if she were wasting her time with useless prayers.

But Jesus's assurances kept her trusting and drove away the temptation: "My daughter, I see everything, I take account of everything. Tell your Mother that I notice every breath that she takes. She must do all within her power to maintain the Chaplet of Mercy.[5]

"I am pleased to see you honor My Holy Wounds; I can now pour out the fruits of My Redemption more abundantly.

"Your monasteries draw down God's graces upon the dioceses in which they are located. When you offer My Father My Holy Wounds, I see you as stretching out your hands to Heaven to obtain graces. Truly, this prayer is not from the earth, but from Heaven, it can obtain everything. You must tell this to your Mother, to remember this and to write it down for the future, so that you might have preferential recourse to it." And

---

[5] "Chaplet of Mercy" and "Rosary of Mercy" are alternate names for the Rosary (or Chaplet) of the Holy Wounds and should not be confused with the subsequent Chaplet of Divine Mercy devotion associated with Polish nun Sister Faustina Kowalska.—Trans.

further: "You are truly blessed, you to whom I have taught the prayer that disarms Me: 'My Jesus, pardon and mercy through the merits of Thy Holy Wounds.' The graces you receive through this invocation are graces of fire. They come from Heaven, and they must return to Heaven."

As the political situation was becoming more critical each day, recounted our Mother in October 1873, we made a novena to the Holy Wounds of Jesus. Immediately, Our Lord expressed His joy about this to the Confidante of His Heart. He then addressed to her these comforting words: "I love your Community so much, no harm shall befall it.

"May your Mother not dwell on the news of the moment, for often the news from outside is false. My word alone is true. I tell you, you have nothing to fear."

Finally, reaffirming the gift of His Holy Wounds to the Community: "Behold your treasure," Jesus repeated… "The treasure of the Holy Wounds includes crowns you must take and give to others… One day, these souls, for whom you will have obtained a holy death by your prayers, will turn to you to thank you. All men shall appear before Me on that day of Judgment and at that time I shall reveal my privileged Spouses who will have purified the world through My Holy Wounds. The day shall come when you see these great things!"

Our Lord's recommendations were not in vain. The custom of daily recourse to this prayer from Heaven has been maintained. And when great difficulties, serious needs, and threatening dangers arise, the invocations are recited even more frequently and with greater urgency. We have recourse to the "Sixty-Six Hundred." This is for us to conform to another light Sister Mary Martha believed she had received from her Master. "You must recite the Rosary in its entirety, because then, all united, you will be honoring the 6,666 strokes of My Scourging."[6]

And after fifty years of experience, the Community can say it has always trusted. It is not that trials spared us or that death spaced out its visits. Far from it. But the trials are tempered with so much consolation. And death is so sweet beneath the shadow of the Holy Wounds!

---

[6] For various opinions on the number of lashes Jesus received during His flagellation, see Carolus Stengelius, *Theatrum D. N. Iesu Christi: atrociorum cruciatuum c. lectori spectatori propositum* ([Augsburg?], 1658), 45-46.

Despite the various well-founded opinions touching on the meaning of the number of lashes during the scourging, nothing prevents interpreting 5,500, 6,000, 6,666 or other similar numbers as having the meaning of "innumerable." It is for this reason that we say: I thank you *a thousand times*, or *infinitely*, so as to say: My acts of thanksgiving are too many to be counted (Note of Fr. Bouchage).

# CHAPTER 11

## SISTER MARY MARTHA
## AND THE CHILD JESUS

IT would be difficult to express the ardent and simple love of Sister Mary Martha for her dear little Jesus, so as to reproduce, as much as one would like, the delightful commerce of their intimacy.

The Child Jesus made Himself visible to her every morning at Holy Communion; but that was unable to suffice for their mutual attachment… Jesus enjoyed the habitual company of this soul in whom, like a clear crystal, the purity and simplicity of the Divine Infancy could reflect itself. Beneath the rustic exterior of our dear Sister, there was in fact something so pure, so fresh, and so ingenuous!

"Her trust is simple and so childlike," wrote the Superior of Sister Mary Martha. "She goes to Our Lord like a small child to the best of fathers."

It is with a real fascination and much interest that one discovers this new distinguishing feature of her moral physiognomy.

To confine ourselves to the aspect principally highlighted up to this point, we would only have a very incomplete knowledge of our Sister's soul: a bit austere in her "mission" of prayer and reparation, the Chosen One of Jesus Crucified was, moreover, a touching example of exquisite intimacy with God, the Most Blessed Virgin, the Saints… and especially the Child Jesus.

Sister Mary Martha shared in the lowly, suffering, penitential, and redeeming life of Jesus Christ. But also, in the company of the Child Jesus, she led the simple, joyful, and sweet life of a child.

These communications, begun at an early age, took on a delightful intimacy within the cloister—with regard to material things as well as things of the soul.

How many times, exhausted or under time constraints, did she implore the help of her little Jesus!

One day when she was unwell and still had not eaten anything at around one o'clock in the afternoon, Sister Mary Martha deliberated whether she should seek out someone to help her with her work, in which she was very much behind: "Good Master, you see where I am with this, what should I do?"

Immediately, a radiant child of six or seven years of age appeared to her: "If you want, I shall come to your aid!"

"Oh, yes Good Master, I am counting on You!"

The Child-God answered, "I am peace's friend and trouble's enemy… I want you to stay close to Me."

With Jesus, and before His divine gaze, everything was soon finished: the table cleared, the dishes done, the sweeping of the choir and the refectory, the preparation of snacks for the students… At two o'clock, our Sister was free for the reading. Jesus remained close to His Spouse until three o'clock, when He disappeared, leaving her in a heavenly joy. At five o'clock, the blessed Privileged One, upon entering the choir, found her dear little Jesus again.

At times, with an unbelievable kindness, the Child Jesus would offer His services: "Give me the command, and I shall do whatever you want."

"Well, my Good Master, help me to do my refectory duties!" And Sister Mary Martha saw the Divine Child before her, doing the cleaning and preparing the tables...

"I want you to continue to do everything for Me," He told her. "Do not ask anyone to help you in your work, then I Myself shall be your help." And He Who has angels for servants went to the sink to start working!...

"The time then passes at lightning speed, while the heart of the very favored Lay Sister is set ablaze with love for her 'divine little Helper, so beautiful... so lovable.' This corner of the house becomes a heaven: the Angels are there, also visible, as members of their Master's court, and our Sister finds that the dishes are finished too soon.

"Always simple, she thinks if some Sister were to pass by at that moment, she would see the Child Jesus washing the plates and her rinsing them... She therefore closes the door so no one suspects what is happening in this blessed place" (Manuscript).

In fact, the Lay Sisters were quite astonished and did not understand how Sister Mary Martha managed by herself to do all the work in a position laden with so many responsibilities. They now know where she got her help from!

We also know there were friendly conversations held there. Jesus would say, "We are living out the Holy Childhood, the two of us... two little children together."

"O good little Jesus, how much do I love you!" she would answer.

And Jesus, appearing happy: "Whenever you will speak to Me like this, even when you won't see Me, I shall be even happier, because I am always listening to you."

As He withdrew, He would ask with tenderness: "My Spouse, are you happy with Me?... Am I helping you well?..."

The scenes that unfolded within the monastery's enclosure were no less graceful.

For our Sister, the time for picking fruit was a time of delight. She continuously conversed out loud with the Beloved of her soul.

Before going to the garden, she would say with simplicity: "My little Jesus, come to work with me, since I cannot stay in the choir with You..."

Sometimes, early in the morning, her dear little Jesus alerted her Himself: "It is time, hurry!..."

She would hurry, carrying two huge baskets to the garden. Jesus accompanied her... She would see Him gathering the fruit with her! With those two, the task was completed in no time and the baskets were filled with beautiful plums!... But how heavy they were!... Sister Mary Martha could not lift them: "Good Master, I cannot carry these large baskets all by myself... but if You help me, it will be fine." Her divine little helper did not leave her in the awkward situation. Both of them returned to the monastery sharing the burden.

Let us move on now to the things of the soul, where there was the same familiarity.

Some of the annual retreats were especially immersed in the light of the Child Jesus's company.

"In order to make your examination of conscience," said the Heavenly Director, in 1878, "you must consider what in your conduct did not conform to Me."

And the adorable Child, revealing and showing His Heart, explained to His Spouse how "in this little Heart was enclosed all the knowledge He had, being older, of His Wounds, of His Passion… and of all the graces He had given her up till now."

The fortunate soul saw with delight the Heart of the sweet Emmanuel and "the little finger on the little Heart of Jesus."

"To believe all these things," the good Master added, "it is necessary to have the simplicity of a child who believes everything told him without reasoning according to human wisdom. A child is trusting with his father and mother because he knows he is loved much and forgiven everything!… I ask you to not waste time during your retreat looking for your faults, but to use the time to contemplate Me."

And on the final day of the solitary retreat in 1885, when the presence of Jesus was even more tender: "If you do not leave Me," the Divine Child assured her, "I shall never leave you."

It was especially at Holy Communion that Sister Mary Martha had to come like a little child to the Father's table: "If you are hungry," Our Lord told His Servant, "come and feed; but to do so, you must be a little child… The soul of a child is a soul without malice, one that is innocent, simple, and trusting. When the soul is in this childlike state, it can come straight to Me; there is no obstacle."

"The heart of this blessed daughter can only think about Jesus," the Superior wrote.

"The sight of the Divine Child, working with her and following her step by step, hardly ever leaves her. She tells us with simplicity: 'Mother, I am as close to Him as I am to you'" (Manuscript).

Feast days for our Sister were ordinarily marked by special favors from the Child Jesus: "Here I am, it is a feast day," He would say. "I come to gladden you, My Spouse!... Learn from this little Child to become like Him, a small little child. This is the grace I give you... Recognize My gifts... See also your misery and never lose sight of it."

"How do you expect me to not see my misery, good little Jesus?" exclaimed the blessed Privileged One. "But be my light, for I cannot keep my promise without You!"

A daughter of St. Francis of Assisi and of St. Francis de Sales, Sister Mary Martha tasted, more than any other perhaps, the feast of Christmas, so dear to her two Patriarchs. The Child Jesus appeared to her then with ever new charms and with such a wondrous beauty that the hours flew by without her even realizing it! She freely surrendered herself to the joys of this contemplation, and the morning would find her in the choir kneeling, in the same position as the evening prior, not having heard or understood anything other than the tenderness of the Divine Newborn.

One year she had the vision of all the Angelic Court and the Blessed surrounding the Manger: "My daughter, to enjoy Me, you must be like those whom you see here... meaning that the earth is no longer anything to you, but that your heart and your mind are always with Me."

Another Christmas night, it was the Most Holy Virgin who brought Jesus to His favored child: "My daughter, I give Him to you; but you must be a little child like Him... Little children want to be with little children."

And the adorable Emmanuel, making her happiness complete, whispered these ineffable words: "If I only had one heart like yours in which to take My delight and all others were ungrateful, I would not regret having come to earth..."

# CHAPTER 12

## SISTER MARY MARTHA AND THE MOST BLESSED VIRGIN, ST. JOSEPH AND THE HOLY FAMILY

### With Jesus There Is Mary

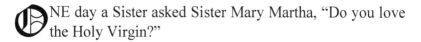NE day a Sister asked Sister Mary Martha, "Do you love the Holy Virgin?"

"Oh, this good Mother, certainly I love her!" she answered, her face lighting up and transforming at this blessed Name, in a radiance of most pure joy.

Profound, indeed, and all filial was her devotion towards Mary. And it was a simple reciprocation, for Mary expressed a most maternal tenderness towards her child.

In going through the manuscripts that relate the favors granted to our Sister, one is extremely touched to see on each page, close to that of Jesus, the beautiful figure of the Immaculate Virgin.

Our lovable Sovereign appeared to her one day in her glory. She inclined towards the earth to look at her daughters and appeared completely mindful of them, without paying attention to the splendor that surrounded her. This good Mother stretched out her hand to our little Sister to draw her to herself (May 3, 1871).

On one feast of the Visitation, July 2, 1878, during Holy Mass, the Queen of Heaven presented herself again to her Servant's contemplation. Overcome with joy, Sister Mary Martha cried out within her heart: "Eternal Father, I offer Thee the merits of the Holy Sacrifice for the greater glory of my good Mother!"

Mary, smiling and "quite pleased" (to use the same expression of this simple soul), told her, "My daughter, you are not mistaken—I am an even better Mother than your Mother, who nevertheless truly loves you!"

This "smiling kindness," by the way, was something Mary wanted to impart to her child. She recommended it to her often: "Your heart must always have a disposition of humility and kindness. My daughter, you are not permitted to think of yourself, but you must continually think of your neighbor."

Another time, Sister Mary Martha was conversing interiorly with her Holy Mother, who expressed being pleased with her: "When a child speaks to his mother in her presence, it pleases her; but when the mother knows the child speaks of her constantly in her absence, she is much happier still."

"Even when it seems you are quite far from me, you are nevertheless still very close. Remember that I am your Mother. Come to me with great confidence and you shall be answered."

And the Servant of God did act in this way. With her, there was never a hesitation or a fear in her appeals to Mary. "When we confided some particular intention to her," recounted the Superior, "and she saw Our Lord was unresponsive to her prayer, she would address the Eternal Father, but more often still, with an extreme confidence, our Immaculate Mother, who would obtain for her the object of her request."

The object of her request was not always of a supernatural order or of extreme importance... At times, the request was simply for good weather.[1] One time this had been asked from Our Lord in vain. Our Sister, turning to the Heavenly Mediatrix, then prayed: "Good Mother, you see that I can obtain nothing; please request this for us."

"On the same day," the manuscript states, "we had very beautiful weather around noontime."

Among the pious practices dear to the heart of our fervent Lay Sister, it is necessary to single out the Rosary. She knew this most beloved prayer. She knew it to be supremely efficacious.

On September 3, 1870, as she was following the Rosary our Sister retreatants customarily recited when walking together after dinner, Mary expressed to her the predilection she had for those who followed this practice: "Those who say my Rosary with fervor will merit to be in my train... Those who make the effort to do this please me."

One day when the entire Community was present at this pious exercise, she was shown the numerous graces and blessings the Savior was pouring on our families as a result of the prayers in honor of His Mother.

"I am the Mother of all souls, but I want to be prayed to," the Most Holy Virgin declared in another circumstance. "You must give me fifteen flowers per day."

The maternal role of Mary is, before all else, to draw and unite souls to Jesus. With what care did she fulfill this role with our Sister!

---

[1] Rain and good weather played a big role in the life of Sister Mary Martha, who, being in charge of the fruit, was concerned about their health.

"My daughter, to spend my month well," she told her on one first of May, "you must continually be recollected inside your heart with Jesus. This is the exercise I practiced my entire life. You must imitate me."

On feast days, she loved to gladden her dear daughter with the sensible presence of the Child-God.

On one July 2: "My daughter, I give you my little Jesus. He will be well accommodated in your innocent heart, which does not know evil."

On one Assumption morning, she said to her at Holy Communion: "He is for you, the little Child, He is for children-souls."

On another day, when placing the Divine Emmanuel in the arms of Sister Mary Martha: "You must carry Him," she tells her graciously, "and ask Him to rain graces down upon the world." The happy child, infinitely joyful, tenderly caressed her dear little Jesus, Whom she pressed to her heart for a quarter of an hour. "Living with Jesus through a childlike joy," the Holy Virgin had explained to her, "is to care for Him in His infancy, it is to participate in the joy my heart experienced when I had the happiness of caring for him at the cradle."

Always the path of spiritual childhood! It was on this path that the Holy Mistress guided our Sister. To this end, she recommended to her obedience: "I do not want you to perform any act, however good it may seem to you, outside of obedience."

She recommended to her purity of intention: "Blessed are the souls who go straight to God with purity of intention, who seek God alone, who do everything for God. They lead on earth the life of the Angels in Heaven!"

She kept her in a state of trust and self-surrender. When Sister Mary Martha was afflicted with a great interior sorrow, her Heavenly Mother consoled, encouraged, and instructed her. "My child, fear nothing, I shall be your guarantor."

"My good Mother, I am worried about the state in which I find myself."

"My daughter, you do not have to worry about your perfection, you only have to do what my Son desires without thinking about yourself... Leave to Him the care of your perfection and you will have everything that is necessary...

"Do not be like slaves—they are always in fear. For you, you must fear nothing, but love much. You are children whose Father loves them very much."

More frequently still, the lesson of humility was repeated on the lips of the Mother of God: "My daughter, put yourself beneath everyone and thank the good God for having placed you amidst such holy Religious."

And the august Virgin seemed to make herself akin to her little Servant, putting herself at her level in order to humble herself: "My daughter, we shall humble ourselves together for poor sinners. Make yourself very little and you shall be my true daughter."

"I can only admire how my Son lowers Himself to such a miserable creature, and I continually ask humility for you."

Sister Mary Martha implored her Divine Mother to obtain for her this invaluable virtue of her Heart. "My daughter," the Most Blessed Virgin responded, "you want me to give you the greatest grace I can grant you, the most pleasing to My Son and to all of the Heavenly Court: humility... I shall grant it to you if you ask me for it every time you have the opportunity to raise yourself up."

"My good Mother," the simple child insisted, "I want it forever."

"There is more love and more humility in asking for it often… You must grow in humility until death—by this means, you will gladden my maternal Heart."

And Mary also made this profound statement, an inexhaustible subject for meditation: "You will become a 'mother of Jesus' like me through humility."

But the Most Blessed Virgin did not want her to forget that her Jesus died *crucified* and that He died *for souls*. She confided to Sister Mary Martha the great desire of her own Heart: "I am hungry for souls! If you only knew how much, with Jesus, I desire their salvation!"

The salvation of souls only occurs through the merits of the Passion of Christ. This was a reminder from His Mother of the "mission" confided to our Sister: "Pray much for sinners so that they receive the fruits of the Redemption. My maternal Heart will be comforted and consoled by this.

"It is in your hearts that Jesus finds reparation through the offering of the Holy Wounds.

"If you wish to please me, you must place yourselves at the foot of my Son's Cross and humbly offer His merits to the Eternal Father, in order to make satisfaction for the sins of men."

The supreme gift of the Virgin Mary, like that of Jesus, while waiting for Heaven, is—after the Manger and the Cross—the Holy Eucharist: "My daughter, I gave Him to you on the beautiful day of your First Communion, and since then, at all of your communions, you see this dear little Child… but on the day of your death, I shall give him to you for Eternity."

Sensing that her heart was quite empty and poor, Sister Mary Martha, before approaching the Holy Table, gladly turned to her good Mother, offering Our Lord the dispositions of this virginal heart to make up for her own. With the most touching condescension, Mary told her one day: "I make myself poor by coming to you, my daughter; together we shall go in this way, poor, to receive my Son; and having nothing, we shall have everything."

Another instance (May 27, 1880), it was in the choir, for the time of adoration, that the Most Blessed Virgin accompanied her: "My daughter," she said, "you must come without your body." Having only just knelt down before the Most Blessed Sacrament, Sister Mary Martha became motionless, her eyes closed, hands joined together, and bearing the expression of a soul who tasted God fully.

During these delightful moments, her heavenly Instructress had her do nothing but offer the merits of the Savior, united with those of His Mother, and continuously repeat to Our Lord for herself and the entire world: "My Jesus, pardon and mercy!"

A very loving child very much loved by the Mother of Heaven—such is our perception then of Sister Mary Martha.

It was undoubtedly a reference to her own qualities when Mary made her to hear these words: "Children-souls who go directly and simply, these are my true daughters."

Our Sister also undoubtedly responded to the ideal traced out for her with that good will that delights a mother's heart, for one day an indescribable thing occurred, something that has the effect of bestowing a new innocence upon a soul: the

Immaculate, inclining towards her humble child, gave her a maternal kiss, saying, "This is how I love you when you love my Son."

### With Jesus and Mary, There Is St. Joseph

Sister Mary Martha's heart did not separate what God had so powerfully and gracefully brought together. She loved "good St. Joseph." To him, she had recourse with filial confidence, following the invitation of the Savior Himself: "You must call St. Joseph your father, for I have given him the title and the goodness of a Father."

And the august Guardian of the Child-God did not despise to come down and converse with our Sister in a sweet familiarity, during which times she received useful instruction for the spiritual life.

Lessons on perfect charity: "My child, Jesus wants your heart undivided. To the extent you are faithful in giving Him all of your love, Jesus will give you a pure love for creatures that will come from Him."

Lessons on recollection and union with God: "I much prefer prayer of the heart and interior union with Jesus than only prayer from the lips."

Promises of help in daily needs: "I take account of all prayers that are addressed to me."

For the hour of death, he gave her this assurance: "If the soul who prayed to me still has debts to pay to the Sovereign Judge, I shall ask for grace on its behalf."

And for every day of her life, he recommended to her the following invocation, which is, incidentally, so apostolic: "Glorious St. Joseph, protect us and protect the Holy Church!"

It was especially *in* the Holy Family and *with* the Holy Family that Sister Mary Martha liked to venerate St. Joseph and to pray to him. *Jesus, Mary, and Joseph*—how she loved to put these three blessed names together! How she loved to contemplate Mary and Joseph with Jesus!

After coming out of a long rapture, she said to her Superior, "Mother, I have come back from Heaven! I cannot say what I saw! I can only say one thing: I was prostrate at the feet of Jesus, Mary, and Joseph. I said to St. Joseph, "Good Father, I thank you for having watched over my Mother Mary while you were on earth… I now ask you to watch over my earthly Mother so that she does not die before I do… St. Joseph did not answer me."[2]

One of her favorite invocations was the following: "Jesus, Mary, and Joseph, I give you my heart, my mind, and my life…" She recited it with so much fervor that she merited this encouragement from the august Spouses: "When you make this invocation, we take your hearts and we give them to Jesus."

"This prayer gives me great glory and great joy," St. Joseph added. "It renews all the happiness that I had in being the Foster Father of Jesus and the Head of the Holy Family."

---

[2] Our Very Honorable Mother Thérèse-Eugénie Revel died long before Sister Mary Martha.

# CHAPTER 13

## SISTER MARY MARTHA & THE MOST HOLY TRINITY

OUR dear Sister had a very powerful attraction to this ineffable Mystery.

From an early age, she was accustomed to doing nothing without invoking the Most Holy Trinity. Prompted to do so by Jesus, she took up the habit of ending each of her works with three signs of the cross, to glorify the Holy Trinity and to make up for the deficiencies caused by routine. It was to the Divine Persons that Our Lord also demanded she promise to completely disclose to her Superior and Directress—despite her repugnance—the graces, lights, and heavenly gifts with which she was favored (Retreat of September 1867).

Sister Mary Martha loved to sum up her devotion to the great Mystery of our faith in the redeeming sign.

"When you make the sign of the cross," the voice from above had taught her, "do so with attention and seriousness, because at that moment the Most Holy Trinity is communicating with you."

We have already seen how the August Trinity manifested itself to the blessed young Sister. One will remember the three great days of September 26-28, 1867, when, in the splendor of the Holy Trinity, God revealed her "mission" to her and traced out for her a course of action for her entire life.

That was the first manifestation. There were others. On one All Hallows Eve, Our Lord had His Beloved enjoy a vision of the adorable Trinity, "Whose feast the Blessed celebrate before their own by contemplating the greatness and majesty of the three Divine Persons." These Blessed, addressing the child on earth, told her: "This feast is full; it cannot be augmented or diminished... It is endless... As for you, you must prepare for tomorrow's feast by delivering souls in Purgatory and paying what they still owe with the merits of Jesus Christ. This is a great work, but it is all joy" (Manuscript).

Another night, as Sister Mary Martha was lying on the floor of her cell crowned with thorns, the three Divine Persons showed themselves to her and she was given lights concerning these words from Genesis: "Let us make man to our image and likeness."

Finally, "one day when Our Lord Himself had been preparing His Servant for confession, about which she had been very anxious, our child again received a visit from the Three Persons of the Holy Trinity. It was as quick as a flash of lightning. The Father told her: 'I bless you and receive you as My child.' The Son told her: 'I give you all the fruit of My Redemption and, in addition to this, I give Myself to you—My Redemption is for the souls whom I confide to you, and Myself, I am for you!... I am your possession.' And the Holy Ghost in turn said to her: 'I come to sanctify you and to sanctify you again.' At that moment, she felt in the depths of her soul such an extreme sorrow for her sins that tears abundantly flowed" (Manuscript).

### God the Father

Towards God the Father, Sister Mary Martha practiced a tender devotion, self-surrender, and the confidence of a child. She felt, she said, "such a great paternity and kindness in this

Creator God, such a great compassion for the misery of poor human creatures, His children!"

She was heard expressing regret that there was no special solemn feast in His honor, and, seeing each Sunday as the day consecrated to His divine rest, she lamented in seeing it so little sanctified in the world.

She loved to address herself frequently to God the Father. Jesus had first invited her to do so, teaching her in His divine manner to say, "Our Father, Who art in Heaven," and advising her to perform genuflections to honor His Father.

Every day, when the word *Pater* was spoken at the table blessing, her soul flew to the feet of the Sovereign Creator: "Good Father, I thank You for all Your benefits. I thank You for having placed me with such holy Religious, and I ask You to bring them all to the perfection of our vocation."

"The simplicity of this dear soul with her good Master and the Eternal Father is incredible," the Annalist wrote, "and through this means she is instructed, consoled, and directed."

"You are like the Father's spoiled and beloved child," Jesus told her, and she knew it well!

God the Father often took her to the beatific realm to be present at feasts that enthralled her. Her soul was thus consumed by ardent longings for the Heavenly Courts.

God the Father taught her to live with Jesus.

One morning, Sister Mary Martha was in choir before the Community had arrived for prayer. Suddenly, her soul saw Heaven open up and the Almighty One incline towards her, telling her with a paternal indulgence: "My child, I give you My Son to help you all throughout the day."

He taught her to live with the Child Jesus, thus encouraging her in this devotion, so full of charm and fruits for her.

He one day recommended that she offer Him Our Lord as a little Child: "Everything is contained in the offering of this little Child. You must often make Me this offering and present."

He also encouraged her in her "mission" of reparation in union with Jesus Crucified: "My daughter, you must humble yourself much in working and offering the Holy Wounds of My Son to fill up what is lacking for My Justice."

"Good Father, if I could so choose, I would go and see you…"

"What would you do in Heaven? You would offer Me the Wounds of My Divine Son. The Saints do nothing else… Your hearts ought always to make this offering with an ardent love."

He taught her to never forget Mary.

One evening prior to the feast of Mary's Nativity (in 1885), waking before midnight to commemorate the birth of the Immaculate Virgin, our dear little Sister heard the voice of the Eternal Father: "My daughter," He said, "thank Me for having given you such a good Mother."

He Himself enveloped her with His paternal tenderness: One evening—it was August 1, 1868—after having her contemplate the Savior on the Cross for a long time and having her experience the sufferings and agony of the Divine Crucified, God the Father stooped down to His humble child and revealed Himself to be so good and so tender that she enjoyed this divine presence for the remainder of the night, having the impression that "only little ones can receive such great favors." And the Heavenly Father whispered: "My child, could you find a comparable happiness elsewhere? This is the compensation for your sufferings. You can always return to Me by making yourself very little in your heart."

### The Holy Ghost

The Holy Ghost *seemed* to hold less of a place in the life of Sister Mary Martha. For her, His action was merged with that of Jesus.

On one Pentecost, Our Lord appeared visibly to His Spouse and, in order to confirm her on her path, told her: "My daughter, the lights you receive come from Me!" And the Spirit of Jesus went into her.

On another Pentecost, Our Lord told her: "My daughter, My Church today received the greatest sign of My love. I have given My Spirit of Light to her." And showing her the Spirit spreading graces and lights over the world, He added: "To receive the fullness of the Holy Ghost, it is necessary to keep your hearts in a state of annihilation and love, like a candle that melts and gets smaller as it is being consumed."

At the same time, it would not be difficult to find the Spirit of Love's distinct "missions" in the life of our Sister.

One must remember she received this Spirit of Love from God the Father in the form of a ray of fire. One will also remember the beneficent visit of the same Spirit, Who had her soul melt in a loving contrition.

Another manifestation that was no less beautiful: Kneeling before the Blessed Sacrament, Sister Mary Martha was just beginning a night of adoration when a magnificent dove, all aglow in light, came to rest above her head, covering her entirely with its wings. At the same time, an ineffable sweetness filled her soul and flooded it with joy. This was a true visit from the

Holy Ghost. "The beauty of this dove was incomparable," our child said, "more beautiful than anything in Heaven."

Whatever these manifestations were, one thing is clear: the power exerted over her soul by Jesus, and by the Spirit of Jesus, had come "to sanctify her and to sanctify her again."

# CHAPTER 14

## SISTER MARY MARTHA & THE HOLY EUCHARIST

OUR Lord established the Sacrament of Love to remain with us and to continue in us the mystery of His Incarnation.

Sister Mary Martha participated in this extension of the Incarnation to a considerable degree. The Eucharist was her daily food from Holy Thursday 1867 until her death, that is to say for close to forty years.

For a period of several years, the Heavenly Bread was even, for the Servant of God, the only food for her body, just as it was for her soul. Let us recall what the Very Honorable Mother Thérèse-Eugénie wrote at the time: "Holy Communion, which is her only food, gives her so much physical strength that she does her very taxing workload with the greatest ease."

Setting her a place at the foot of the Tabernacle like at the foot of the Cross, Our Lord made clear to His Spouse that it was there she would find the best of her strength: "My daughter, if you did not climb Calvary each day in spite of your suffering and if you did not come to receive Me each morning, you would not have the strength to work. Holy Communion is your life!... It is the means I employ to make you capable of serving the Community. Without this grace of daily Communion, you would be spending your life in bed."

"Holy Communion and suffering—these are your food, these are your two meals."

This divine food was her body's strength, because it was first of all life, the strength of her soul... What a beautiful Eucharistic soul was Sister Mary Martha's! In this soul, what a hunger for the Eucharistic Jesus!...

It was only in Him that she found her support and her consolation. In between Communions she longed for the next, and when she approached the Holy Table, one sensed she was running to the Founts of Life. Her face then took on an appearance of calm and recollected joy, utterly remarkable for those who could catch a glimpse of her. One could see in the transparency of her face the love of a heart possessing Jesus: "I hold Him Whom my soul desires, and I shall not let Him go."

"Towards morning," the manuscript states, "Sister Mary Martha feels herself strongly drawn to God and, sometimes, at the moment of Communion, she hears the voice of Jesus calling her: 'Come quickly, My Bride! Come and do what the Blessed are doing in Heaven... come receive Me in Communion to enjoy Me...'

"'Good Master,' the blessed child says in a transport of joy, seeing Jesus in her and sensing herself in Him, 'Good Master, I hold You, You are everything to me.'

"'Yes,' answers the Savior, 'I am everything to you!... Take Me with you... I shall work with you.'"

Such words inflamed her with love and all her days were spent in an intimate and sensible union with her beloved Jesus.

This ardent love made the least delay very difficult for her, and certainly the least suspension.

After the death of Canon Bouvier, the new confessor for the Community wanted to make no exceptions during a retreat and imposed on her, as was the custom at the time, a few days without Communion.

The Savior's humble Privileged One obeyed without murmur, but her pain was such that she was seen fainting upon exiting the confessional.

A pious lover of the Eucharist who was acquainted with the ineffably tender sentiments of her Divine Master, she liked to say: "The time seems long to Our Lord on the eve of Communions, so much does He desire to enter our hearts."

Let us mention an incident that demonstrates what price our Sister sometimes paid to content the Heart of the Heavenly Bridegroom.

"On Sunday, December 31, 1871, after Conventual Mass, Sister Mary Martha, trembling with fever and no longer able to hold herself up, was forced to stay in bed. She remained extremely unwell for three days. Our Lord came to visit her each morning; but on the fourth day, He made known to His Bride that He would not come, and that if she wanted to receive Him she had to go to Him.

"Filled with a spirit of faith, our Very Honorable Mother Marie-Alexis permits her daughter to obey the Master's good pleasure. Despite heavy perspiration, Sister Mary Martha begins to dress herself. Her weakness is so great that she falls, half-fainting. The infirmarian is obliged to get her back up and to help her finish getting ready to go out. With the help of the Superior, she takes her to the area in the church for the infirmed, where the poor sick one slumps into a chair, looking like someone who is close to death.

"She hears Mass and is given Holy Communion. Scarcely had she received Our Lord when her strength returns to her. Her thanksgiving completed, she returns to her duties and, on this same day, performs all of the work in the students' refectory" (Manuscript).

One could say that all of our Sister's life was but a preparation for Communion and a prolonged thanksgiving.

Humility, purity, detachment from all created things, and simple and loving trust—these were the dispositions which, through His graces and teachings, the Divine Master maintained in His faithful disciple.

"Good Master, what will you find in my miserable heart?"

"My daughter, I shall find everything I have put there. I shall also find your faults to annihilate them. However, to do so, you must truly be alone with Me in your heart.

"When coming to Holy Communion, you must bring the ardor of the Angels and the humility of My Mother."

"Hurry to me like you are starving," the Savior said another time. Not knowing what she ought to do, our ignorant child questioned her Master. "My daughter, it is by profoundly abasing yourself through humility; this is also the only means of making Holy Communion fruitful."

After receiving the Holy Eucharist, Sister Mary Martha sensed her heart so closely united and bound to the Heart of Jesus that she was unable to express the power of this union, and we know how she delightfully lost herself in this adorable Heart.

Jesus, however, told her one day: "There are some who eat of this Bread infrequently and know how to profit from it well...

You who feed on it so often, you do not know how to profit from it!"

"Oh, Mother," she admitted sighing and with sincere humility, "it is so true! Our Lord is always with me... How far I am from knowing how to profit from it! But I have prayed to the Blessed Virgin, our Holy Founders, and the good Angels to make up for what I am lacking... and they have promised me this!"

These were words of humility. We know how much Our Lord took delight in His Bride. He taught her how to make a good thanksgiving just as He had taught her how to make a good preparation.

"My daughter, give Me your heart to thank Me for Holy Communion and I shall grant you new graces for the satisfaction you will have given me.

"I am in your heart; do nothing but look at Me, and for My part, I shall look at you, and the entire day we shall be together. This is your thanksgiving!"

One November morning, Sister Mary Martha, obligated to leave choir for a work of absolute necessity, did not dare to do so before the end of the prescribed time for thanksgiving. Her good Master reassured her with these words: "Go, My child, I only want and look at the heart. You can do your thanksgiving anywhere. The love of My Heart is constantly active with yours."

In all of this, our dear Sister hardly thought to do any self-analysis. It was necessary to question her to get her to reveal her interior sentiments and attitude towards Jesus.

One day, her spiritual helper[1] asked her what method she used
when hearing Holy Mass. "Always the same," she answered, in
language that calls to mind that of the Holy Curé of Ars. "I
follow Our Lord in His Passion... I see Him before His judges.
They mistreated Him so much! He is slapped, pushed, and then
thrown to the ground. There are some who pull him by the hair
to the right and to the left. They tear at His beard... Oh, how He
is made to suffer! And He, always meek, He lets everything
happen... And with Herod? He is dressed in a white robe, they
mock Him—in all kinds of ways. O my Jesus! My Jesus!"

As Sister Mary Martha talked, her speech became choked up
like someone crushed with sorrow: "After the flagellation, He
falls to the ground, all torn, all covered in blood... And the
prison! And the crowning with thorns!..."

Enumerating the sufferings of her good Master in this way,
as if they were truly before her eyes, tears flowed down her face.
She eventually burst into sobs, saying in a broken voice: "Oh, I
cannot speak of this! O my Jesus! My Jesus!"

"And Your Charity sees this every day?"

"Yes, every day up until the Elevation. Then it is the little
Jesus," she said as her face lit up. "It is the little Jesus until
Communion, when I receive Him. It is unspeakable, but it is
Paradise. Oh, how happy one is! When we are both together like
that, the hours go by like minutes."

"The hours go by like minutes." Yet temptation finds a way
of inserting itself into this happiness to disturb it.

---

[1] "Spiritual helpers," whose roles are likened to those of "angels" by St.
Francis de Sales, meet once a month to encourage each other in the love of
God and to correct each other's defects.

The divine flowers of grace are always interwoven with cruel thorns, and the most holy desires of this soul encountered contradictions! Contradictions, doubts, fears, and perplexities. Contradictions also in certain dealings with creatures.

One sometimes witnessed a pious jealousy, joined to a certain astonishment, at the favor granted to our Sister, the favor of daily communion, which was very rare at that time. "You ought to be a saint," she was told, "you who receive communion every day!"[2] The humble Lay Sister maintained her silence: was not her secret pain a powerful feeling of unworthiness? The imperfections had not disappeared from her life and they naturally manifested themselves at times in her daily occupations! The thought of her communions thus became for her a cause of great interior pain. One understands if her neighbor's remarks increased this pain!

But Our Lord did not allow her to stop. One day, Sister Mary Martha was tempted to refrain from Holy Communion because of what people might say. Jesus reproached her for this: "My daughter, would you deprive souls of the great good they receive from your Communion?… Your communion is reparation to Me for ungrateful hearts that offend Me and for those who receive Me poorly… And you would dispense with it out of self-love!"

Her Superior recounted that on another day, as her soul was again greatly troubled, our dear Sister did not dare to approach the Holy Table. However, full of faith in the word of Obedience given her, she overcame her fear. Jesus welcomed her with kindness: "My daughter, tell your Superior it was the greatest

---

[2] It is necessary to mention in passing that after the decree of His Holiness Pius X, when the Community enjoyed the great happiness of feeding each day on the daily Bread from Heaven, Sister Mary Martha permitted herself an innocent retort: "Well, Sisters," she asked, "what do you have to say about it now?… Are you saints?"

act of charity she could do in having sent you to Communion. Come to Me, My daughter, for you are ill in two respects. First, you suffer the privation of God and must come to Me to be healed. Secondly, you also suffer from your nothingness and misery, which constitute a great void needing to be filled by Me!"

## *Visits to the Blessed Sacrament & Eucharistic Vigils*

"If we love Our Lord," the Holy Curé of Ars says, "we should always be mindful of the Golden Tabernacle, this House of the Good God. When we are traveling and catch sight of a church bell tower, this sight ought to excite our hearts… we ought not to be able to withdraw our gaze."

Such indeed was the love of Sister Mary Martha for the Eucharistic Jesus. Her heart and her eyes were always directed towards the Tabernacle.

When she would have her conversation[3] in the garden, close to the chevet of the parish church, she would never consent to sitting with her back towards it. Throughout the day, even amidst absorbing occupations, the thought of the Tabernacle remained habitually on her mind.

Our Lord insistently beckoned her there: "I instituted My Sacrament of Love to be the companion of man," this Good Master told her. "You must constantly sustain yourself with Me and continually speak with Me heart to heart. Speak to Me, look at Me!… This is what you will be doing for all Eternity! Here is found the soul's food, true rest, and the soul is in its center."

Appearing to her on the Cross and showing her the Blood from His Divine Wounds: "Everyone passes by, and no one

---

[3] The monthly conversation with her spiritual helper.

looks at this Blood!… Similarly, in My Sacrament of Love, one thinks of Me for a moment, and then I am forgotten!

"My daughter, I am here just as much as in Heaven… I keep Myself in the Tabernacle for your love, and so few souls come to visit Me!"

Corpus Christi and Holy Thursday, with the visits to the altars of repose, were days our Sister welcomed with joy. Her joy, however, was mingled with the heartbreaking pain of seeing the Eucharistic Jesus so little understood and so little loved. The complaints of the Divine Prisoner moved her deeply: "At the altars of repose, I keep silent as in the stable in Bethlehem. A multitude of people will come to visit Me, some of them out of mere curiosity and others out of vanity—such souls offend Me. It is for you to make reparation to Me through your recollection and silence."

And insisting on this duty of reparation, which permits the Divine Heart to pour out the excess of its graces: "When I find a heart that loves Me and makes reparation to Me, I take My delight with it… That is why, My daughter, I want your nights like your days to be occupied with this holy exercise."

We know how our Privileged One's Eucharistic vigils were spent.

When it was time for others to rest, she was beginning a second life, unknown to the Community, a solitary life at the feet of the King of Love. There, Sister Mary Martha would contemplate and would offer thanks. Above all, she would pray and make reparation.

She especially prayed for sinners and for the souls in Purgatory, standing, in a way, at the gate of Paradise, to have souls enter therein through the merits of the Savior's Holy Wounds.

Fatigue, disgust, anguish, and diverse temptations were not absent from these hours of watching, no more than they were absent from the rest of her life.

Nevertheless, more often than not she was the object of the most tender caresses from the Divine Master, who treated her like another Margaret Mary. Our Lord, all while keeping hidden His workings in this humble Bride, seemed to want to grant her the rarest and loftiest of graces... To her also He showed His adorable Heart, a burning furnace... He snatched her own heart to immerse it and melt it in this fire of love.

Thus, the Superior continued, Sister Mary Martha physically felt her heart taken out of her and its space left empty. In her naiveté, she told us, "Mother, until this morning I did not know that the heart was on the left side." More than once, Jesus renewed this divine robbery.

The holy vigil sometimes took place at the choir door or in a small nook of the monastery church rather than in the tribune: "I see you wherever you are," the Beloved then said to her. "It is not a wall that can prevent Me from communicating with you."

And another time: "I Myself make the breach in the wall separating us to come to you as a little Child." That evening He was of such a wondrous beauty that her soul was so beside itself with love. The rest of the night passed quickly like a flash of lightning, in a Heavenly joy: "Now," announced the Good Master, "I put in this place everything that can make you happy; later I shall only put here disgust.

"You must obtain graces through suffering, like the Blessed obtain them through love."

Such a prospect was not likely to surprise or frighten our Sister. Had she not, for her part, chosen suffering in union with the Master? She preferred the company of the Immolated Bridegroom over all of the raptures: "My nights with Jesus Crucified are the most delightful," she admitted. "It is then that I feel the most encouraged and consoled for later bearing the work and suffering of the day."

During these vigils, whether they were imbued with suffering or joy, Our Lord often deigned to play an active role. He would outline the night's agenda, suggesting successive intentions. Or He would even ask questions to stimulate fervor or provoke love: "My daughter, what are you doing here?"

"Good Master, I am here to behold You and to thank You."

"And I," Jesus responded, "I am here to grant you new favors!"

After having her pray for several hours and having granted her a last look of love, tender like a mother who sees her child's exhaustion, the Savior ordered her towards morning to go lie down: "Now, it is finished, you can go rest" (1868).

This happened rarely, for despite the work and sufferings, the Lord of the Tabernacle ordinarily wanted her as company in His solitude.

One evening, Sister Mary Martha was ill and exhausted, with no energy left. Our Very Honorable Mother ordered her to ask Our Lord for sufficient health to do her work well. Jesus answered: "If you want to spend the night at My feet, the strength will be given you." Authorized by her Superior and despite the trembling of exhausted nature, our Sister acquiesced to the Divine Will. On the next day, strength and good health returned to her.

The Sovereign Master also enabled His little victim to appreciate the grace of His demands: "I have two lamps that burn here before Me," He told her one evening, "but the one I take greater pleasure in is you.

"See, My daughter, what honor I give you in keeping you at My feet. You are here to conquer My Heart and to keep Me company for your entire Community.

"You are very blessed, for I give you much time to love Me. I give you the day and the night; however, I shall also demand an account of this time…"

Additional precious encouragements came to revive Sister Mary Martha's fervor. The voice of God the Father made itself heard, sweet and caressing: "I associate you with My Angels for adoring My Son and keeping Him company."

And St. Francis de Sales added: "It is a great honor for me to have one of my daughters associated with the Angels for adoring Jesus and practicing charity by praying for men…"

A kind of admirable emulation established itself between the Angels and our Sister.

"We have only our spirits and you have your bodies," the blessed army said, "your bodies which glorify our God through each one of their actions… your bodies which must be like blazing lamps, burning and being consumed everywhere and always, at the service and for the love of our good Master."

It was especially at the foot of the Blessed Sacrament that the dear adorer made her body, as her soul, a holocaust of love… remaining on her knees, motionless, in contemplation of Him Whom she loved exclusively.

And for Sister Mary Martha the Eucharistic influences continued even when she was away from the choir. How could she forget these words from Jesus: "The Tabernacle—you must take it with you everywhere!"

# CHAPTER 15

## SISTER MARY MARTHA
## AND HER COMMUNITY

WE know no better way to crown this first part of our work than by following Sister Mary Martha in her Community and at the Boarding School.

In the same way that we already know her with her moral temperament, her "mission" of expiation, and her delightful familiarity with Heaven, so do we also find her here in her everyday surroundings.

In the immense family of the Institute, the "Community" is a small family greatly loved. It is here that each Religious was welcomed, adopted, and formed; here that each one grew in the school of the Holy Founders, in the knowledge and love of Jesus the Bridegroom; here that very close bonds of supernatural charity were formed with a venerable Mother and choice Sisters that continue after death. The love of the Community is imbued with a special tenderness that is joined with gratitude and veneration.

All of this was present in Sister Mary Martha's affection, in her "veneration" of the Community in Chambéry.

To a large extent, she owed this to the strong lessons of her Mistress, our Very Honorable Mother Marie-Alexis Blanc. In her talks with the novices, the latter never tired of speaking of the affection, respect, and gratitude owed to the Community "which did us the kindness of receiving us." She vigorously called attention to any failings or negligence regarding this point. She taught: "In everything and before all else, one must consider the Community... In our duties, we do not look at ourselves, nor at our own convenience, but at the well-being and interest of the Community... Let us not seek to spare ourselves pains when it is a question of the Community... In the places where the Community gathers, there should be respect, courtesy, and deference, not inconsideration or carelessness... If the Community is to gather in a place, let everything there be in perfect order!... The *Community*—this word must hold you spellbound!"

This kind of rhetoric etched itself indelibly in the hearts of the novices.

There was no one these words penetrated more than our fervent Lay Sister.

In her Community, the most ordinary things as well as the most elevated things—material interests, meeting places, traditions, spiritual goods, Sisters and Superiors—everything was as sacred to her.

The Community, how much Sister Mary Martha loved it! She was not indifferent to anything that pertained to it.

We could perceive that she suffered in seeing herself normally deprived of familial gatherings, which are so sweet in religious life. Thus, when a great feast day brought her a respite, or especially when boarding school vacation suspended her customary work, how joyfully we saw her arrive among us and offer her services to her white-veiled companions!

Visiting the sick was a joy for her. With few words, but with delicacy, she expressed to them her sentiments of sisterly affection and compassionate concern. And when one of them was at the point of dying, she prayed and suffered for them with an incomparable zeal and devotion, albeit unknown.

She lived with her Community in the Hereafter… We shall later see the charitable relations she maintained with the dearly departed.

And what to say about her love for her Mothers! "For our Mother," assured Sister Mary Martha, "I would do anything, I would let myself be killed!" She could not see them in pain without consoling them: "Good Mother," she sometimes said, "I am pained because your heart is in pain."

To her Community she belonged, giving it her energy to the point of exhaustion, offering her prayers day and night, and her unceasing sacrifices.

Prayers and sacrifices! This brings us back to a trait of her physiognomy that is already known. What our Sister was for the entire world—an intercessor and a victim—she was foremost for her Community.

"Do you see, My daughter," Our Lord told her at different times in 1866 and 1867, "you are charged with the flock just like I am… Each day you must pay the debt of each soul in this Community towards My Justice… I hold you responsible for your neighbor's faults… Each day you will be the victim to expiate the sins of them all."

She was given similar counsel during these same years by our former Mother Marie-Pauline Deglapigny, who, on July 30, 1873, would further specify and complete the earlier messages.[1]

---

[1] Recall that Mother Marie-Pauline Deglapigny died in 1866. She communicated this message to Sister Mary Martha from the other side of the grave.—Trans.

"When a Mother has seen what the Justice of God demands from the souls of religious for such small faults that easily escape them, she ardently desires to see them freed of all debts when they come to the moment of death. I have asked God this grace for you: so that no one leaves this life without having paid off what they owe the Divine Justice, that someone in this Community be charged with making up for what they lack, and it is you who have been chosen—that is why, when someone is to die, you will suffer much. You must not forget this."

Sister Mary Martha thus saw herself as entrusted, in the Community and for the Community, with a mission of prayer and expiation. One will recall her act of offering, which clearly specified:

"I promise Our Lord Jesus Christ to offer myself each morning to God the Father, in union with the Divine Wounds of Jesus Crucified... *for the good and perfection of my Community.*

"I promise Our Lord to offer every ten minutes... the Divine Wounds of His Sacred Body to the Eternal Father... to unite all my actions to His Holy Wounds... *for all the needs of my Community, those of the Novitiate and the Boarding School, and in atonement for all the offenses committed therein.*"

God seems to have truly accepted this "oblation" if one judges by the blessings which followed it.

On October 8, 1868, Sister Mary Martha was designated to replace the Sister gardener, who was then making her annual retreat: "My daughter," the Divine Master told her, "today I shall make Myself a gardener with you." While she was working, Jesus suddenly appeared before her in the way He had showed Himself to His disciples after the Resurrection. Revealing the glorious Wound of His Sacred Heart and stretching out His arms to His humble Servant, He told her with inexpressible tenderness: "Give Me your heart!" As she zealously offered it to Him, she sensed that He accepted it and that, full of love, He enveloped it in His own: "Now your Community has Me entirely!... This union is not only for you, but for all the members of your Community."

Jesus took her in spirit throughout the monastery, promising His blessing to each employment: "You will tell your Mothers that they should fear nothing, I love them too much."

On multiple occasions, the Good Master repeated these same assurances:

"In your needs, you must pray and I shall give to you... You must live in gratitude and self-surrender... You must not worry about anything, other than loving Me and thanking Me, then I shall take care of everything."

And yet on another day: "Go over in your mind all the souls in your Community and ask Me graces for each one of them... Your Community does not know the treasure it possesses. I tell you: As long as it has its treasure, it has nothing to fear!...

"My daughter, it is I within you Who am this treasure." And she was clearly shown that everything was enclosed within her perpetual offering of the Holy Wounds of Our Lord Jesus Christ.

"We had great difficulty getting these words out of her," the manuscript notes. "In her extreme embarrassment, she had to exert considerable effort to articulate them."

However, at the same time, the manuscripts testify to the graces received. At each moment, the pen of our venerable Mothers was gushing with gratitude for the protection that visibly surrounded our Community.

We find in the monastery annals, for the year 1873, a note written by our Very Honorable Mother Thérèse-Eugénie, who was Assistant at the time. It was an outpouring of the heart, attesting that "only in Heaven shall we know how much God loves our religious family." This was a veiled allusion, which is now perfectly clear to us.

In fact, in the documents relating to Sister Mary Martha, the same Annalist declared: "It is impossible to enumerate here all the graces the Community receives by means of this humble daughter who lives unknown amidst her Sisters... We truly perceive an evident supernatural assistance around this blessed child. Everything put in her charge prospers. Everything entrusted to this simple soul is multiplied in a way that recalls the oil and flour in Sarepta and the small inexhaustible barrel of La Galerie.[2]

On March 7, 1868, Our Lord sent His little Servant to bless the supply of potatoes that was coming to an end. He commanded her to get on her knees and humble herself and then to make three signs of the cross "in the Name and to the glory of the Holy Trinity." The humble Lay Sister knew at that moment that the Holy Trinity had received her prayer. In the evening, she told us: "Mother, you must believe that there will be potatoes to last us all the way through. Our Lord said so." Indeed, contrary to all human expectations, the rather small pile no longer diminished, although one drew from there each day the considerable amount needed for the Boarding School and the Community. There were some there until the new ones... They were so good that, in eating the last of them in the month of June,

---

[2] "La Galerie" is the name of the house that was the cradle of the Visitation Order, where a barrel of wine given as alms to the Religious in 1610 miraculously lasted until the following year's wine harvest. See Émile Bougaud, *Histoire de Sainte Chantal et des origines de la Visitation*, 9th ed. (Paris: Poussielgue Frères, 1879), 1:434.

the Community mistook them for Marjolin potatoes, given how fresh they were. Our cooking Sisters did not know what to think or say: "This is truly extraordinary—there has been a miracle" (Manuscript).

On July 19, 1885, Sister Mary Martha had done an abundant and thorough harvesting of raspberries. On the following day, it was time for the plums. As she was filling the baskets, she felt urged interiorly to go back to the raspberries. "But, my Jesus, that is of no use," she replied. "Yesterday I took them all, there are no more." Feeling the interior prompting even stronger, our good Lay Sister finally yielded to it. What a surprise to find branches bending from the weight of big, beautiful raspberries!

"My daughter, I placed them here to give you the pleasure of offering some to your Sisters…"

"Oh, thank you, good Master! It will be necessary to put as much next year."

Our older Sisters remember with admiration the prodigious quantity of fruit that the garden provided at the time. Our Lord, it seems, was pleased to multiply them because His chosen one was in charge of harvesting them: "You are the little child of the family that is sent to the harvest," He told her, "and the Master puts everything that is necessary there for you to find."

During a retreat, our Sister had to take part, out of obedience, in a group harvesting of grapes. This was not without much cost to her. "Now," states our Very Honorable Mother Thérèse-Eugénie, "it happened that our dear child filled nine baskets in a place that was already visited… Astonished at everything she gathered, we said to her, 'But where did you get all of this from?' She answered, 'Indeed! I don't know how it happened. As soon as I would pick a bunch, I would notice another next to it.'"

A similar cause for astonishment, at another time, led to these remarks from a Sister gardener: "How is this happening? There is nothing to be seen on the trees, yet every day Sister Mary Martha fills baskets of fruit!"

One time there was a shortage of lamp oil in the House. In desperation, we went to the Servant of God. Although she had not replenished her own supply, she found that her container was so hardly tapped into that she had the satisfaction of providing for her Sisters.

When the wine in the barrels was souring or the potatoes in the cellar were rotting, obedience sent Sister Mary Martha to bring remedy. Arming herself with the sign of the cross, she invoked the Blessed Trinity and Our Lord's Sacred Wounds. The wine would again become excellent, and the spoiled portions of the potatoes would dry up, the rest being preserved.

Those of the Religious who, on account of their particular jobs, had witnessed the damage, were dazed in astonishment and, not knowing to whom to attribute these prodigies, thought they must be due to the holiness of their Superior.[3] As for our Mother, she wrote down everything and kept silent.

***

It is especially with respect to spiritual goods that we owe much gratitude to our dear Privileged One.

"God alone can appreciate and number them," we read in a manuscript. This is the attestation of the Superiors, who alone knew, and who summed up their thoughts in this way.

---

[3] The Institute's circular *Vie de notre T. H. Mère Marie-Alexis Blanc*, dated 1891.

The Community itself did not know. But despite the marvels of grace working in our dear Sister being unknown, one generally had a special confidence in her prayers, which one sensed must be very pleasing to God; thus, in moments of hardship, one willingly commended oneself to her intercession. And then, through a look or a word, the pious Lay Sister brought the relief needed by the suffering soul.

"A young Sister asked her one day: 'What must I do, Sister Mary Martha, to have the good God spoil me a little?' Sister Mary Martha fixed her eyes on her interlocutor for a moment. 'Never,' declared this Sister, 'never will I forget that look!... It seemed to me that those wide-open, clear, scrutinizing eyes were looking into the deepest recesses of my soul. I experienced an indefinable sensation, which was all the more moving given that one so rarely saw the dear Lay Sister's eyelids go up. After a few seconds, which seemed long to me, she answered me with an authority that was both sweet and compassionate: 'Little Sister, you must see *only Him*!... You must think *only of Him...* love *only Him... nothing but Him!*'"

"To the same question, another Sister obtained this answer: 'Sister, one must *really humble oneself...* really, really humble oneself!'"

"These counsels," our Mother added, "were truly God's almighty word for these souls!" (Manuscript).

Our Superiors especially—one understands why, and we have already mentioned it before—loved to have recourse to their dear child when a difficult event threatened the Community.

And, sensitive to the prayers of His little Privileged One, the Divine Master often deigned to reassure them through her humble mediation: "I am the Guardian of this Community!... I shall always protect it," He said with extreme kindness.

The assurances of preservation multiplied with the dangers. As early as the month of August 1870, Our Lord had this word conveyed to our Mother: "Tell your Superior to be without worry—the evil shall not approach you..."

On February 29, 1871 [sic], He renewed His promises of safety: "The devil is enraged against the Community, because herein is a source of graces through the devotion to My Holy Wounds. Your Community is like a vessel on a raging sea, but it shall not perish—I am its Captain."

In 1873 and 1878, there were new assurances: "I know each of My Brides by name... I so much love to behold those who are faithful to Me."

"Good Master, if you know us all, will you watch over us well and will you preserve our good Father Bouvier for us?..."

"I shall watch over you in your monastery, I shall give you My peace, and I shall still preserve your good Father, because he is necessary for you."[4]

These assurances became more frequent in 1880. During the Octave of Corpus Christi, as Sister Mary Martha was renewing her supplications, the Child Jesus deigned to appear to her and, putting His finger on His Heart, said: "My daughter, even though this Heart will not tell you at every moment that It is watching over you, it suffices that It has told you once. You will have many reasons to fear, but do not be afraid, little flock... I have promised to watch over you."

---

[4] Fr. Bouvier, who was in his seventies at the time, was ill. He recovered and was with us for another seven years.

On May 8, 1881, our Sister was in the garden, very preoccupied with the harvesting, which was shaping up very beautifully, but also with events which seemed more threatening than ever. She asked God to let us enjoy the beautiful fruit which He had so liberally given us: "See, good Master, how nice everything is here!... and the wicked want to destroy everything."

Suddenly, Our Lord appeared before her, full of majesty and kindness. "My daughter," He said, as He made a protective gesture over the entire enclosure from its summit, "the wicked look, but I Myself am keeping watch."

# CHAPTER 16

## SISTER MARY MARTHA AND THE BOARDING SCHOOL

THE Boarding School! Its mention evokes memories of a bygone era. But an era whose remembrance remains fresh, like that of the pleasant youth whose cheerfulness then enlivened our cloister.

We have already mentioned how, owing to an imperial ordinance, the Visitation of Chambéry was reestablished at the beginning of the last century.

Our Boarding School, which opened on September 30, 1806, would last until April 1904. It was clearly not in the mind of the Holy Founder and it harmonized rather poorly with the strictly contemplative life. But circumstances had made it a necessity. And our Mothers, who regarded teaching as a kind of immolation and apostolate, did not believe, consequently, that they could evade "this task imposed by Providence and the voice of our Superiors."[1] Moreover, the Boarding School was, before all else, a house of formation—one was more concerned about providing a moral and religious upbringing in the Salesian spirit than about mere academics and the conferral of diplomas. Many women, accomplished in every respect, learned there the secret

---

[1] The Institute's circular *Vie de notre T. H. Mère Marie-Alexis Blanc*, dated 1891.

of an exemplary life. And for how many souls was the Boarding School the gateway to the Convent!

It was in service to the students that Sister Mary Martha spent almost the entirety of her religious life. In entrusting her with the job of boarding school refectorian from the time of her novitiate, it is assumed that the Superiors chose it over all other jobs for favoring the action of God in this Privileged One, since her life was thus being spent in greater solitude. Somewhat on the peripheries of the Community,[2] it also pulled her away from the attention of her fellow Sisters and enabled our Mothers to more easily converse with her.

Beginning in 1866, the figure of Sister Mary Martha, a young professed of twenty-five years of age, appeared in our boarders' pleasant and cheerful surroundings. Then the years passed, with the gaggle of students always returning. Each year the same Refectorian was there to welcome them, always just as active, just as devoted… until the day when, painfully resigned, she saw the door close to the children, never to open to them again!

---

[2] The boarding school occupied one wing of our buildings—the same one as the choir, which was separated from the students' refectory by a wide corridor. Nearby was the great cloister of the monastery, to which opened the children's recreation room, which was also part of our Sister's domain. By the refectory entrance was a narrow space for the Servant of God to wash and store the dishes, which also served as her oratory. The old statuettes and simple paintings there received her respectful homage.

The infirmary, where Sister Mary Martha had her bed, and the tribune (looking out onto the church interior) are on the upper level.

None of the former students—the correspondence testifies to this—can think back on their time as young boarders without remembering "good Sister Martha!"[3]

This "good Sister Martha," they did not refrain from teasing her! They made fun of her naïveté, and they at times abused her patience. The virtuous Lay Sister went along with it all without abandoning her usual simplicity and benevolence.

"Sister Martha, what color was Henry IV's white plume?"

"Oh! Miss, you'll need to ask your teachers. I didn't go to school…"

"Sister, have you read *Don Quixote*?"

"Miss, I don't know how to read."

"Oh, what a pity! It's such a beautiful book! You could have requested it for your retreat!"

The students at times subjected her to real affronts, in order to obtain bigger pieces of fresh bread or chocolate. And one can imagine our gourmands' mirth when they were given the answer: "Oh, misses, you must learn to eat whomever!"

---

[3] The Holy Wounds pamphlet was the occasion and starting point for a considerable amount of correspondence. First came letters from our former students recalling, with their memories of the dear boarding school, that of the humble Sister Refectorian. The least disciplined in times past are today the "proudest" to have "best known" Sister Mary Martha. One of them who is well-known in Lémenc declared, upon the publication of the Notice about the Servant of God, that no one was more entitled to it since no one else became so close with the good Sister. Dining almost every Sunday in the little nook adjacent to the Refectory as a "penance," she assures us she "enjoyed" the simple rooster feather bouquets with which the pious Lay Sister would decorate the statue of the Blessed Virgin in winter.

Oh yes, they teased Sister Mary Martha. But how much they loved her! And what influence did this very simple Religious, assigned to a menial job, exert on the souls of these young girls! Merciless judges at times, but very perceptive ones, they intuited her to be of outstanding virtue and proclaimed her a saint! "Sister," one of them said, "it seems that you see the good God." Another observed: "When you are sick and they replace you, things don't go as well." They saw the efficacy of her prayers in the details of boarding school life. They confided certain personal troubles to her, and Our Lord gave His Servant words that were so full of the Spirit of God that they made a profound impression. They already envisaged her in Heaven: "Sister, when you're in Heaven, remember that… at that place…" What happened between that student and Sister Mary Martha? We did not dare to ask her, the Superior noted, so as not to seem to attach importance to the matter.

What we knew, our Mother added, was the visible blessing that God desired to grant the Boarding School from the time our little Privileged One was assigned to this post. Here also, there were amazing things that ought to be mentioned. Such as "the miracle of the wine."

As the Refectorian, our Sister had to prepare the wine destined for the children by mixing it with water. Her heavenly Director ordered her to trace three times on the bottles thus prepared, in honor of the Father, and of the Son, and of the Holy Ghost, the sacred sign of our Redemption. She made this her custom. It was June 1867. From that time onwards, there was such a multiplication that our Very Honorable Mother Thérèse-Eugénie did not hesitate to compare it to the "miracle of the wedding feast at Cana." "One liter of wine," she wrote, "and sometimes a smaller quantity, suffices for the meal of fifty to sixty students."

Much later, the pen of our Very Honorable Mother Jeanne-Françoise Breton would write these lines: "At the beginning of each school year, Sister Mary Martha came to ask her Superior if she ought to begin again to prepare the beverage for the Boarding School in the way that Our Lord had taught her. And the same grace was always granted, on condition that permission was not withdrawn from her to continue the austere life she had been leading for so many years. We tested this out ourselves."

"This is not," Jesus told Sister Mary Martha, "for economizing on wine that this grace is granted you, but on account of the glory that redounds to the August Trinity from this act done with such faith, humility, and innocent simplicity."

To the rest, God allowed this matter to pass almost unnoticed. Sometimes the Refectorian had to be replaced in her duties, and the Sister in charge of the cellar contented herself with remarks such as this one: "I don't understand any of this! When Sister Mary Martha serves the students, hardly any of the wine gets used up…"

Various healings also attested to the blessed influence of the dear Lay Sister. Let us look at the manuscripts:

"A student was seized with a very severe bout of fever. The illness had made such rapid progress that the little sick one's condition became very worrying. Sister Mary Martha, charged with watching over her, prayed nine *Memorares* with faith and confidence. On the following day, the child was healed."

One incident that was yet more striking occurred in March 1881.

"One of our students was in bed for two days with a raging fever. Worried, we had our Privileged One pray for the cure of our little sick one. Upon finishing her prayer, the child was instantaneously cured and asked to get up and eat… We could not believe our eyes—it seemed like she had never been sick! She immediately went to class, and no one would have suspected how sick this student had been. The Sister Infirmarian was in deep astonishment; yet, from our hearts, a thousand thanks went up to God for such a favor."

It need not be pointed out, since it is so evident, that the devoted Refectorian did not limit her preoccupations to the material aspects of her position. Always immersed in the supernatural, she especially thought of the souls of "our children" in her comings and goings. To them, at every moment, belonged her prayers, her sacrifices, and her solicitude.

Moreover, Our Lord continuously nurtured in her thoughts of apostolic zeal. Manifesting the sentiments of His Divine Heart so as to have them animate the heart of His docile disciple, He revealed to her how much He loved our young students. Once when the students were returning to start a new school year, Jesus said: "I take much pleasure in seeing the students coming. They are my little flock, it is I Who watch over them." And on another day: "Love them like I do."

Seeing, in the light of God, the children's pure consciences, and the benefit of the good formation, which cast the solid foundations of true piety into their souls, Sister Mary Martha thanked Our Lord and became attached to our students with a touching affection.

Let us listen to her confess in simplicity to her "Good Master" that—overcome undoubtedly with this feeling of tenderness— she raised her eyes at Mass during the Gospel "to see those dear little ones." Let us also hear Jesus leading her back onto the wondrously fruitful path of sacrifice: "If you do not watch them, I shall watch them Myself, and I shall bless them."

"Take Me everywhere in your work, so that the students find Me there," He said to her on another day.

For her, He even deigned at times to honor the students' refectory with His sensible presence: "We are coming to the feast," He said with kindness.

In a period of aridity, after three days of painful interior desolation, our Sister, moved by an intense desire, uttered this cry of the heart to Jesus at the beginning of a meal: "Good Master, You are invited to the Visitation's wedding feast here in this refectory."

"I come to you," answered the Savior, "not only with My Mother, but I also bring along a great host of My friends if you so desire." She then saw the Most Blessed Virgin and numerous Saints, and then the Guardian Angels of our students. Our Lord looked at them all with kindness. The vision lasted as long as the meal, without taking from Sister Mary Martha her freedom of spirit. She continued serving, her soul inundated with joy, without anything revealing itself externally, except a more profound recollection and a heavenly countenance (April 9, 1869).

Our Lord also deigned to encourage His Servant and, through her, the Superiors and Directors: "The Boarding School gives Me great glory through the religious principles and good formation the students receive."

Such a result evidently implied the fine qualities of the teachers: "This job demands much abnegation and a great inner spirit.

"The children take to the world all of their boarding school memories—you must, therefore, tend much to your students' souls.

"The Teachers must strongly urge them to remain faithful to frequenting the Sacraments, despite the world's difficulties and lazy nature. The frequenting of the sacraments will be the only means of salvation for some; without this, there are some who will not persevere."

Jesus expressed His satisfaction with the students' devotion to the Holy Wounds: "I await the students' return, for they glorify Me on account of the Holy Wounds. During vacation, the students spread the devotion…"

He was interested in their little practices of mortification: "The dry bread at their snack time[4] was more difficult for them than your fasting was for you."

He was interested in their health: "I shall take care of the children… I keep them constantly before My eyes, one by one. I tell you this so that you pray to Me for them."

One year, at the time of Easter vacation, our Mothers hesitated to send the children away due to an epidemic that was rife in the city: "The One Who sustains the health of the children will know how to preserve them from epidemic diseases during their two days away."

On Holy Thursday, April 6, 1871, Our Lord further insisted: "I want it noted that for the five years and two months that your bed has been in the infirmary,[5] there have not been any serious illnesses." This bed in the infirmary was hardly used by our Sister, as her Divine Master ordinarily wanted her before the Most Blessed Sacrament. It was as though He had an interest in His Servant not being obliged to watch over sick children!

---

[4] During the [Franco-Prussian] War of 1870.
[5] The boarding school's infirmary.

On the eve of First Communions, as during troubled times, the Savior had Sister Mary Martha pay, so to speak, for the graces destined for the boarding students—the prayers had to become more fervent and the cross weighed more heavily. That was part of our Sister's "task."

What was also part of her "task" was the care of accompanying beyond the grave with her prayers those of our students whom God had called to Himself, and to likewise follow with her prayers those who, each year at the end of their studies, returned to their families… and to the worries of life.

She never failed in this regard. And now, those who have survived her gladly raise their eyes to Heaven in times of trial to still ask help from "good Sister Martha."

# CHAPTER 17

## FAITH, PRAYER, GRATITUDE, SIMPLICITY, TRUST & SURRENDER

SISTER Mary Martha did not write. She did not have scholarly conversations about spirituality. Therefore, to speak of her virtues does not mean disclosing her thoughts; it means especially, if not solely, seeing her act, seeing her live under Our Lord's action. Considered in this way, she is truly admirable—we have already been able to realize this in the course of the preceding chapters.

These chapters have sufficiently brought to light certain general traits of her spiritual physiognomy so that it would be needless to dwell on them much longer. Every page shows Sister Mary Martha to be a soul of faith and prayer, a thankful soul, a simple, trusting, and surrendered soul. We will only recall these things before touching on other virtues especially pertinent to the religious state: humility, mortification, the vowed virtues of chastity, obedience, and poverty, charity, and apostolic zeal.

Faith is the fundamental basis of any Christian life. God wanted to firmly establish it in the soul of our Sister.

It truly seems that from the moment her eyes opened to see earthly light, they also opened to the lights of faith. The precious seed planted in her soul at Holy Baptism developed magnificently, to the point that she fathomed, in an astounding manner, the mysteries of our religion: the adorable Trinity, the

Incarnation of the Word, the Redemption, and the Holy Eucharist became clear to her with wondrous light.

Moving in this light, Sister Mary Martha had the faith as her motive and guide from an early age, in her acts and in her thoughts—she lived only for God, acted only for God, and saw only God in all things: "God is here, God sees me, God hears me."

It would be this way for her entire life, as she sought the glory of God and lamented at the remembrance of the sins of men, who outraged with their crimes the majesty of this God Whom she adored! With what ardor she desired to cooperate with the Savior Jesus for their salvation! How much she longed for her blessed home, where she would forever be reunited with the object of her faith! She accepted sufferings and expiations, in order to obtain this happiness for the poor souls in Purgatory. What fervor she brought to her prayers for the Church, the world, her homeland, and her Community! With what reverence and humility she approached the Holy Sacraments!... What love for Jesus Christ! What devotion to Mary, her tender Mother, to our Holy Founders, the Angels, and the Saints! And what signs of the cross in honor of the Blessed Trinity!

This same spirit of faith guided her in her relations with her neighbor and, especially, in her relations with authority. Whatever the word from the priest or her Superior, her simple childlike soul avidly embraced it; she believed in it more than in her own lights. But we shall speak of this elsewhere.

From such a living and practical faith naturally flowed, as from a wellspring, prayer.

Sister Mary Martha prayed like she breathed. Her family still remembers how this child would get up at night to pray in secret. Later, when her young nieces would come to see her in the monastery, the pious aunt would have only this one recommendation on her lips: "You see, my little ones, you always have to pray. When you are walking, you need to take your rosary and say it. When you go to the fields, you must offer your work to the good God. This way, nothing is lost." And after some edifying words, Sister Mary Martha dismissed them: "I do not know what more to say to you now."

Our dear Sister, in fact, hardly knew how to converse with creatures. But how adept she was at conversing with God! Like a thurible of burning incense, she breathed forth sweet perfumes of love at the feet of her Beloved.

It was because her Master was the Beloved Himself!

Sometimes Our Lord reminded her of the unremitting precept of prayer, be it vocal, mental, or of action.

Sometimes He prompted her to pray according to His preferences. "Good Master, what prayer must I do?" she asked one day when coming before Him.

"My beloved daughter, do the prayer that I taught you, that of heart to heart with Me. No prayer is more pleasing to Me; it is of more worth than prayer of the lips… I want prayer from the heart."

Sometimes He emphasized the beauty and power of prayer: "Prayer is the way to go to God and to find Him. Heaven and earth meet through prayer; justice gives way to mercy…"

Docile to the teachings received, Sister Mary Martha was, as we have stated earlier, the monastery's "perpetual Intercessor." And we know how pleased God was to graciously hear her.

But also, with respect to such a good God, our Sister was so full of gratitude!

Gratitude! Jesus wanted to see it in his Chosen One in a very special way. He carefully placed and cultivated this exquisite flower in her soul.

One of the Privileged One's sufferings sprang from man's ingratitude. God gives so much! We thank Him so poorly and so little! Her heart was always in a state of thanksgiving, just as it was always in a state of love and reparation. Everything provided her an opportunity to raise her thankful heart to the Heavenly Father: the fruits and vegetables she gathered, the rain, the sun, fire, food, the gifts of nature and still more those of grace… Everything invited her to praise Him.

One of the practices she was fond of was giving thanks for the chief benefit of the Redemption.

Another practice was to give thanks to the Eucharistic Jesus in the souls of communicants returning from the Holy Table.

Softening the blows of ingratitude and forgetfulness made to the Heart of Jesus by assuming, in accordance with Our Lord's request, "the responsibility of gratitude," was also among Sister Mary Martha's noble ambitions.

In her Eucharistic vigils, thanksgiving was continuously joined to prayers of reparation and contemplation.

And, for herself, she gave thanks not only for ordinary graces and pleasant benefits, but also for painful and crucifying graces. The good Master directed her thus: "You must receive My blows with joy and say, with each pain, 'Thank you, my God!'"

Truly, if gratitude is one of the signs by which beautiful souls are known, what a beautiful soul was that of our humble Sister's! "Pardon, thank you!"—how often did these words spring from her heart to her lips!

"Sister, what must one say to Jesus?" she was sometimes asked. She answered, "Only these words: 'Pardon, thank you!' But you must say them always."

Sister Mary Martha's spirit of faith, prayer, and thanksgiving was characterized by perfect simplicity. And this was one of the charms that attracted the Heart of the Divine Bridegroom.

"Simplicity," according to St. Francis de Sales, is nothing other than an "act of pure and simple charity that has but one end: to acquire the love of God; and our soul is simple when we have no other pretention in all that we do."[1]

Our Sister had no "other pretension" than that. Her purity of intention attained that degree where it becomes "the gaze of the creature seeking the gaze of God."

"Gaze upon Me," Jesus told her, "for I am always looking at you... This is the face of a God Who watches you. When I have a Bride, I always have My eyes turned towards her... Gaze upon Me to imitate Me, and I Myself shall gaze upon you to purge you of your misery." Sister Mary Martha responded to this loving provocation from the Bridegroom. Entire hours passed this way, especially during the night vigils. "Your gaze is enough for Me," said the Beloved, "and I Myself gaze upon you."

It was a gaze of contemplation and love which persisted in times of external activity, and whose sweet and spontaneous admission Jesus found sweet to elicit. Appearing one day to His Privileged One as she was sweeping the great cloister of the monastery, He asked: "Are you doing this for My divine gaze?"

"Yes, good Master!"

---

[1] Conference 12.

For those who came close to Sister Mary Martha, this gaze of her soul solely towards God did not pass unnoticed: "One sensed," one of her companions said, "that there was nothing natural in her, that she did not look at herself." She did not look at herself because—like the servant described by the Psalmist[2]— she sought in God alone her course of action, without human consideration or turning in on herself.

Her disposition was all the more pleasing to Our Lord because it was imbued with an innocent candor. Her Superior attested, "She truly has the candor of a child. We asked her, regarding the favor she enjoyed of seeing the Child Jesus each day in Holy Communion, 'Did you ever, when you were in the world, speak of this to your Confessor?'"

"Oh, no, Mother, I thought everyone saw the same thing."

During the period when Our Lord asked her to make three signs of the cross to keep the potatoes from spoiling, Sister Mary Martha once foresaw that she would be unable to go down to the cellar again on the following day. "Here are three for tomorrow, if You want them, my Jesus."

In the month of September 1885, she was harvesting figs, by order of her Superior. She lost her balance at the top of a ladder and grabbed onto the branches, crying out: "Good Jesus, hold me, our Mother entrusted me to You."

Simplicity, candor, and perfect straightforwardness thus penetrated her life to the point of becoming a very prominent feature of her physiognomy.

---

[2] Psalm 122.

Simplicity in her relations with God, with the Superiors, and with her neighbors. Simplicity of life, of demeanor, and of disposition.

We cannot imagine anything in Sister Mary Martha that resembles posturing or affectation, not even out of embarrassment or human respect. Nothing about her was forced or stilted. After her ecstasies, she simply returned to her ordinary occupations without appearing to be self-conscious.

Nothing complicated in her interior life: duty, the will of God, service to the Community, love of Jesus and Mary, prayer for everyone—these were her sole objectives.

Truly, Jesus could say to His Beloved: "I have fashioned your heart to My liking and for Me. I have removed from it all glances towards the creature. I have placed therein great gratitude, which makes it remember My benefits. I have placed therein the simplicity of a child."

He took great care, moreover, to maintain and develop this virtue of simplicity in His Chosen One. And especially in her relations with her Superiors, His demands went very far.

One day, the Child Jesus appeared to His little Servant, so beautiful and so lovable that she was plunged into an indescribable rapture. Desirous of keeping all this joy to herself alone, she promised herself interiorly not to speak of it. Immediately, the Divine Child reproached her for this: "I love little children who resemble Me and say everything with simplicity. The true child tells his Mother everything—likewise, My daughter, you must tell your Mother everything."

He once asked her to give a message to the Superior and she delayed in relaying it. Appearing as a very small Child (our

Sister assured us she saw Him with her eyes), He asked her in a serious tone: "Which of the two of us is bigger?"

Astonished, Sister Mary Martha answered, "Good Master, bodily, I am bigger than You; nevertheless, I am nothing before You." Our Lord then made her to understand that there was a reproach in His question—she had made herself "the bigger one" by not promptly complying with the Divine Will.

Reproaches of this kind did nothing to lessen Sister Mary Martha's trust. She had too well understood this lesson from the Master: "The path of love and trust is the one that I love to see My Brides traveling. The other paths are less certain and more difficult."

For our Sister, however, trust was not without difficulties. Her delicate conscience and her ardent love for Jesus would have inclined her to grieve at the excesses of certain purely external failings. Furthermore, if Heaven's favors were generously lavished upon her, let us not forget that she had to also experience moral anxieties, uncertainties on her path, and the harassment and even furious assaults of the devil.

In these painful moments, her refuge was an unshakable faith in God's goodness and the words of His representatives. Armed in this way, Sister Mary Martha triumphed over all attacks and maintained her simple and serene trust. Did she not have, moreover, as a supreme refuge, the very Heart of her Beloved? Indeed, if Jesus had chosen His victim and "crucified" her in a thousand ways, He made sure, on the other hand, to defend her from any excessive fears: "Throw yourself into My arms," He told her. "There, one cannot perish. I do not want you to have the least mistrust. I want love, not fear."

Favored with daily Communion, our Sister hesitated at times to approach the Holy Table: she believed herself too great of a sinner. "My good Jesus," she said one morning with anxiety, "our Mother wants me to go to Communion."

"Come to Me then without worry," the good Master answered. "Be like the little chick that closes its eyes, concealing itself beneath the wing of its mother."

One day in September 1875, our Sister was, more than usual, being tormented by the devil. As she continued working, she began to sing in her characteristic manner in a show of defiance to the enemy: "O Eternal Father, I offer Thee the five Wounds of Thy Son Jesus to obtain for the world and our Sisters the healing of our wounds and the deliverance of the Holy Souls in Purgatory." This voice, which was hardly harmonious to the ears of creatures, penetrated Heaven... Jesus, hearing these tones, ran quickly to comfort His Bride, telling her of "the value and beauty of such a canticle."

An infidelity having plunged her into grief, Our Lord told her: "Come then to Me—you are a little child... A father does not take offense, a father does not look at the 'follies' of very small children. I love little children, I love souls who come to Me with confidence after their faults."

"My daughter," He told her one day, "I am with you day and night, present in your heart, and I shall stay here without interruption as long as you carry on as I desire: little, lowly, and entrenched in your nothingness."

In her simplicity, our Sister asked: "My good Jesus, when I commit faults, how is it You stay with me?"

"You are like the child who offends his father without knowing it," answered the Savior. "Once he realizes it, he runs to his father, who forgets everything."

It seemed to Sister Mary Martha that her union with Jesus was all the closer and more perfect because her misery was that much greater: "My Jesus, I await everything from You alone, for I am only misery."

When it expresses itself with such humility and faith, trust is called surrender.

Self-surrendered, our Sister did not have much trouble being in mundane circumstances—she loved Our Lord so much that she sought His good pleasure in everything, always ready to sacrifice the divine consolations of prayer for the obscure and toilsome labor of her work.

But along a path strewn with painful trials, total and unresisting surrender beneath the hand of God sometimes demanded genuine immolation.

In the years of fasting called for by the Master, there were hours when the poor child, feeling exhausted, had the instinctive impression she would die of weakness. What generosity and self-surrender were thus required of her to conform herself to Our Lord's counsels: "Do not worry… Await from My good pleasure the signal to return to the refectory."

It was the same in the crucifying perplexities of her extraordinary path, with its succession of humiliations and pitfalls… To be Jesus's "plaything of love" comprised all of this, and Sister Mary Martha docilely was just that.

She confessed to her Superior: "Mother, I see that Our Lord is ever more Master of myself—I do not do what I want, but what He wants."

Did our dear Sister have to struggle much to get to this point? Was the progress slow or quick? It is not easy to answer…

Whatever the case, it seems she advanced very far on this path so dear to the Holy Founder.

Five or six months prior to her death, according to her spiritual helper, we asked her whether she feared death or desired it. With an expression of intense desire, as if she had already tasted the delights of divine union and eternal beatitude so many times, Her Charity exclaimed: "Oh, I would love to die!" Then, immediately correcting herself: "But... I prefer the Will of God. Living or dying is nothing, as long as I do the Will of God."

"Yes, I understand. But does Purgatory not frighten you?"

"Oh, well, I don't think about it, I am resigned. Let Him do His Will; for my part, I am resigned!"

# CHAPTER 18

## THE HUMILITY OF SISTER MARY MARTHA

HUMILITY was indisputably Sister Mary Martha's fundamental and dominant virtue. Such was the testimony of everyone who knew her. "At her death," wrote our Very Honorable Mother Jeanne-Françoise Breton, "her companions were unanimous in paying homage to her rare humility."

It seems that Our Lord especially predisposed and solicited her on this point, and particularly assisted her with this. There were few things where grace's role was more manifest.

We have already heard some of the appeals from the Divine Master. They could not be more pressing: "My daughter, if you do not humble yourself, you will not follow the path that I have traced out for you to come to Me.

"All the glory of the kings of the earth is here below; and although all glory is due Him, Jesus only sought His in humility and pain...

"You will not be a true Bride if you do not love being humbled." And moving on to the positive corollary, He added: "You must have no other desire than to be scorned and treated as you deserve."

Our Lord often gave His Servant clear knowledge of the good within the souls of her Sisters, setting it in contrast to the picture of her own misery.

"I cannot do with you everything that I want; and even for a great part of what you are doing, it is your Superiors making you do it... But I always choose the most miserable creatures to spread my gifts..." And the Savior invited His Bride to immerse herself in the salutary conviction of her own nothingness. Pointing her to the source from which she must draw this virtue so dear to His meek and humble Heart, He lovingly said to her: "Steep your soul inside here. Come like the turtledove to hide yourself in this sacred hole, and I shall cover you with a mantle of humility!"

He further emphasized humility by showing it to be the condition and pledge of divine favors: "When a soul humbles and empties itself, it attracts Me like a magnet attracts iron!... I left My glory, I humbled Myself, I made Myself very little to come to you... and you, to be ready to receive My graces, must empty yourself much, for I regard only the humble heart!"

This was to mark out for her a magnificent program. Sister Mary Martha knew how to conform herself to it. She carried herself in humility to attract Jesus with His graces; and Jesus, coming with His graces, increased in her the thirst for humility—this summed up everything. From contact with Jesus, she maintained this humility which is, according to Father Faber, "the perfume of God" and "the token the Creator leaves upon the creature when He has pressed upon it for a moment."[1] Our Lord having Himself given her this instruction of admirable depths, "My Heart only works through the charm of humility," she was aware of the need to speak and act accordingly.

On January 1, 1870, our dear Sister was by the boarding school refectory, busy washing the dishes, when Heaven

---

[1] Frederick William Faber, *The Foot of the Cross, or The Sorrows of Mary*, 4th American ed. (Baltimore: Murphy & Co., 1859), 208.

suddenly filled the humble space. The Visitandines and a host of the Blessed appeared to her. In a transport of joy, the pious Lay Sister cried out, "Do you want to give Our Lord a message for me? Tell Him that I am… a sinner."

After a night during which she suffered much physically and mentally, feeling exhausted and incapable of tending to her duties, Sister Mary Martha remained at the choir door. It seemed to her that, in this spot, she would have easier access to the Master. And there, profoundly humbling herself before His Divine Majesty, she said: "Good Master, I am Your poor one. Give me alms, give me strength."

One day, our dear Sister had been continuously offering the Holy Wounds of Our Lord for the conversion of poor sinners. She then had the inspiration to go to the feet of the large miraculous Christ[2] and to humble herself in the name of all creatures. The sweet Jesus welcomed her with tenderness and told her in an ineffable voice: "My love receives this act of humility as if all of my creatures had actually humbled themselves at My feet."

Heaven's favors only penetrated her still further with the sense of her own misery. "My daughter," her Divine Master taught her, "when I bring you down, you must humble yourself much; but when I raise you up by giving you My graces, you must humble yourself even more."

The manuscript notes, in fact, that each time this dear soul was obligated, out of obedience, to give an account of what was advantageous to her, as well as of the graces with which she was favored, it was for her an extreme embarrassment, a real martyrdom!

---

[2] See chap. 1, n. 9.

Such sentiments regulated her attitude, not only before God, but in all the details of everyday life.

Our Lord continuously maintained her, firmly, in humility, both interiorly and exteriorly.

To the Assistant Sister who questioned her about her intimate relations with the Divine Master, Sister Mary Martha confided with a charming simplicity: "When I have lacked humility, He goes into hiding and does not return until I have put things right… There is only to humble oneself, to make oneself little to have Him return! Oh, how He loves that!... So, I cannot not ask pardon, I must ask right away, right away!

"One cannot live without Him!... When I have displeased our Sisters, if I have been rude, if I have stood my ground, the little Jesus goes away… Oh, how sad that is!... I go to the choir and I don't find Him… So, I leave, I look for the Sister, I ask pardon and… He comes back!... We cannot live apart, the two of us!..."

"Yesterday, entering the vestibule, I left the door open, because a Sister carrying something heavy was coming behind me. Another Sister passed by and closed the door. I went back, opened the door again, and said, 'Some common sense! Don't you see that a Sister is coming and has her hands full?' I had scarcely said these words, and the little Jesus went away. I no longer had peace, and I had to ask forgiveness. I looked for the Sister and only saw her when she was entering the refectory. Quickly I told her, 'Forgive me, I am a proud woman.' After that, I had more peace… but it was only at the Obedience, when I asked pardon at the time specified by the Rule, that the little Jesus returned."

One sees here, by the way, in what Sister Mary Martha's defects consisted. There was at times a lack of external decorum, when her natural vivacity overtook her, or a certain insistence about an idea she believed beneficial for the common good, or a manner of acting that astonished because her true motives were unknown. As for the seriousness of the faults, it did not go beyond an initial impulse. Never did our good Lay Sister talk back in a proud or hurtful manner; never did she say a word that might offend her neighbor, still less one expressing any resentment or selfishness. And always, let us repeat, the reparation took place in an edifying manner. This is what the Very Honorable Mother Jeanne-Françoise noted: "She truly made herself exemplary in the practice of this item from the Directory and recommended it to the young Sisters who asked her the way to please Jesus."

Our Sister's personal fidelity on this point was not always, in its perfection, free from annoyance to her neighbor. Thus, one day, believing she had shown a lack of respect to the Sister Cellarer, she went looking for her shortly before mealtime: "Pardon, Sister."

The poor Officer, extremely busy, found the apology untimely. "But, Sister, now is not the time!"

"Pardon, Sister, pardon," continued our humble Lay Sister, still on her knees. Feeling increasingly tested, the dear Cellarer turned to another Sister who was a silent witness to the little scene: "You see, Sister Mary Martha, you are also testing Sister N.!"

Sister Mary Martha simply and meekly responded: "Oh, Sister N., she loves me!"

"Words," Sister N. added, after the death of our Privileged One, "that remain with me as a very sweet memory."

There are other testimonies to cite. Here is one from a Sister who was a longtime Assistant of the Community: "What struck me more in our relations as 'spiritual helpers' was—along with the purity, candor, and simplicity of soul—Sister Mary Martha's so rare and so profound humility. She seemed to be steeped in it. We could always address certain exterior failings, forgetfulness, etc. Lowering her head with a look of contrition and shame, she would say: 'It's true... it's very true, Sister Assistant!... I will try to do better—I am so crude!'" (She always used the expression "crude," which, on her lips, meant uncultivated and unrefined.)

"Sometimes, her Charity seemed to 'stand her ground,' as she used to say. We never had the impression that there was any voluntary stubbornness in it; she believed she was following her conscience and her duties."

"She followed her conscience!"—a remark that is very beautiful, very precise, and that brilliantly casts light on the soul of Sister Mary Martha.

A white-veiled Sister, full of veneration for her companion, for whom she was also a spiritual helper, also sought to penetrate the secret of this soul. She affirmed having no doubt that her Charity "was fundamentally humble and always very faithful to her conscience and to the views of perfection, insofar as she understood things!"

In one incident, Sister Mary Martha had been a little too insistent with a Sister and received some rather mortifying words in response. She did not delay in coming back and offering her thanks: "Sister," she said humbly, "you have enlightened my conscience..." Thus, her understanding had only lacked some enlightenment, and she was full of gratitude towards anyone who showed her her defects and her duty.

Even the graces God gave her were occasions for growth in humility... What little rebuffs and painful remarks she had to endure when, having been rapt up in God, she came too late for our Sisters' liking to help them in the kitchen! "Oh, that's convenient," it was sometimes said, "one stays quietly in prayer and leaves all the work to others." Likewise, there were good-humored words that made the dear Sister very embarrassed: "What a beautiful hymn our Sisters sang at the Exposition of the Most Blessed Sacrament!"[3]

"There was singing?" asked Sister Mary Martha, involuntarily betraying the secret of the Bridegroom, Who had enraptured her senses.

"What? You didn't hear anything?... Oh, of course, Your Charity was still in ecstasy!" How embarrassing for our Sister! She kept silent, blushing, and visibly suffered from being the focus of her companions' attention.

One day, after a similar episode, a Choir Sister who was coincidentally passing by took pity on her and wanted to console her: "Let them talk, my good Sister Mary Martha... all of this means nothing and will not prevent you from enjoying the delights of Our Lord."

But, her sadness becoming still deeper, Sister Mary Martha meekly replied: "Oh, Sister, can one be certain?... Is it truly Him?" Her humility made her ever fearful, steeped her in the deepest silence, and prevented any self-satisfaction for so many divine favors.

Suffering from erysipelas, which kept her in the infirmary, she piously made use of her free time reciting, with a sick companion, the dear invocations she received from the Savior's own lips: *My Jesus, pardon...* and *Eternal Father, I offer*

---

[3] At nocturnal exposition for one of the feast days when we enjoyed this favor.

*Thee....* One Sister, who had little inclination to the Holy Wounds devotion, or rather to the inauguration of the new prayer, interrupted her in a rather spirited tone: "You mustn't say it like that, Sister... You won't gain any indulgences. You must only say, 'My Jesus, mercy.'" Immediately, Sister Mary Martha humbly acquiesced and continued her prayer saying only: "My Jesus, mercy."

There was another similar incident, this time in the kitchen. Our Lay Sisters were gathered together and were about to begin the invocations to the Holy Wounds when one of them asked: "But why do we say 'pardon and mercy'?"

"That," another carelessly replied, "is an *invention* of Sister Mary Martha's."

This time, her face showed a little bit of annoyance. "But these invocations are very pleasing to Our Lord," she said, and then she reimmersed herself in her usual recollection.

"Never," added the Sister who recounted this incident, "never did Sister Mary Martha say anything of the graces received. One joked with her at times. When there was a question about mystical states during a lecture, those of her companions who somewhat suspected the 'secret of the King' ventured to say, 'You know all about this, don't you, Sister Mary Martha?' And our good Sister let out a wholehearted laugh—that was her only response.

"Once the story of a saint who had gone a long time without eating was read aloud in the refectory. Not knowing that such was the case with our dear Sister, I approached her when leaving the table and said, 'This saint went a long time without eating anything.' Sister Mary Martha kept silent for a moment and then continued with recreation."

When the Very Honorable Mother Marie-Emmanuelle de Gand[4] visited our Monastery in 1904 on her way to Revigliasco, Her Charity specifically asked to see our pious Sister, whom she had known about for a long time through the accounts of Reverend Father Ambroise and the letters of our former Mothers. The meeting lasted more than an hour. We know that the dignified and holy Superior held the humble Lay Sister in high esteem. The latter subsequently told our Sister Assistant, with earnest admiration: "Oh, how humble she is, this Mother!... How humble she is! You wouldn't believe it! She asked me if I thought Our Lord was happy with her!" And our Privileged One did not even think for a moment that this questioning might reflect the high regard in which she was held!

Not only did Sister Mary Martha keep silent about the divine favors of which she was the object, but she even seemed like a stranger to spiritual knowledge—so much did she maintain herself in obscure lowliness. It must be said that, from the beginning of her supernatural graces, our venerated Mothers had recommended she not speak of her prayers—as simple and innocent as our dear Sister was, she would have unwittingly betrayed herself.[5]

---

[4] Superior of our monastery in Romans. In this dear community, they still remember the words of Reverend Father Ambroise concerning the "Privileged One in Chambéry": "Oh, Sisters," the fervent friar said in conclusion, "it is *costly* to be a saint!"

[5] One might be astonished here by some confidences from Sister Mary Martha to one of us, mentioned in the course of our account. We would be astonished as well if we did not see it as a special permission from God. When, in 1906, our good Lay Sister learned she was assigned our Very Honorable Sister Assistant as her spiritual helper, she appeared somewhat shocked: "I really believe I am going to die soon," she said to her dear Sister Marie-Jacqueline, "because I have never had a Choir Sister as an Angel..." Perhaps she had had a premonition of these words that subsequently escaped her, so to speak, in the course of a more intimate conversation.

One had tried to elicit some devout words from her. The one to whom Jesus revealed His most intimate secrets did not know how or want to say anything... She had but one saying on her lips: "Sister, it is necessary to humble oneself... to really humble oneself... in that is everything!"

"Sister Mary Martha, I am in dryness, tell me your way for getting Our Lord to come."

"Oh, that is not difficult... One need only humble oneself!... One must humble oneself, humble oneself!!!" she repeated, as the expression on her face seemed to add: "Oh, if one only knew what a treasure it is for the soul to be able to humble itself—that is the key to all graces!"

Sometimes, however, by way of exception, Sister Mary Martha gave more details to conform herself to Our Lord's desires. Our Very Honorable Mother Thérèse-Eugénie believed it necessary to note, among other things, the following advice: "Here is what Jesus inspired His little Servant to say to a servant girl who was to be admitted for a trial period: 'When you are in the novitiate, don't believe you are above the other servant girls... Conduct yourself with them in total humility... You must always put yourself at the feet of everyone and believe that if you do any good, it is with God's help... Being approved of, say it is God Who did everything. If you are disapproved of, put yourself in agreement with your neighbor and humble yourself still more!... Then you will have everything you need to be a good Religious. Being humble and working in the sight of God—that is everything!" (August 1869).

---

Furthermore, let us add that Our Lord, jealous till the end of keeping His humble bride hidden, permitted that, all while giving full credence to the confidences of Sister Mary Martha, our Sister Assistant not attach much importance to them at the time.

These words now seem to us especially well placed, addressed as they were—we have reason to believe—to one of our deceased white-veiled Sisters, whose keen intellect, skillfulness, and tireless dedication were to be useful to the Superiors and the Community. Jesus wanted, no doubt, to guard her against the pitfall of vain complacency. So many precious gifts were to subsequently merit her successes, praises, and words of satisfaction.

Such was not the case with Sister Mary Martha. One might believe that, being favored by Heaven, she must have also been favored by the Superiors. The contrary is the truth.

From the beginning, her Mistress, our Very Honorable Sister Marie-Alexis Blanc, while admiring the work of God in her Novice, guided her with a firm and forceful hand, and made it a course of action to humble her constantly.

With perhaps the exception of our venerable Mother Thérèse-Eugénie, the Superiors did not spare her in public or in private, and sharply rebuked the slightest oversight or least appearance of imperfection.

But the rod of correction fell upon an unfailing humility.

Sister Mary Martha's physiognomy, at such times, took on an appearance of extraordinary jubilation, which was joined to a profound self-annihilation... One had the sense looking at her that she entered into herself, disappearing, so much did her outward attitude convey the sentiments of her soul. Moreover, this appearance of self-diminishment and self-annihilation was her normal expression, which she maintained even in times of great activity. Yet when she encountered correction, she became inimitable. Some young Lay Sisters were almost jealous of it and said to her: "So that doesn't upset you at all?... You savor the admonitions like a delicacy..."

"Oh, it's a little thing; it is upsetting, it turns everything upside down inside; but I don't dwell on it... it does the soul so much good... and that is pleasing to Him!"

Her heart did not feel any less acutely the little frictions of community life, which were perhaps more frequent for her on account of her underdevelopment in "human and earthly things" and her lack of refinement in external interactions. But she bore all these frictions with generosity.

"No matter how cordial she was," said one of her young companions, "she was often received poorly." During the students' vacations when she would volunteer her help to the cleaning Sisters, her kind offers were not always welcomed gracefully: "Go pray... we don't need you."

Confiding in her spiritual helper about some minor work difficulties, Sister Mary Martha simply added: "Well, of course, on earth, we're not Angels!... We know it well, and Our Lord does also!... We're not Angels! This saying always does me good—it's my brother who told it to me.

"After the family property was divided up, my brothers came to see me. I said to them: 'So, brothers, is everything settled now?... You didn't quarrel?'

'Oh, it's all settled. But it's true—we did quibble a bit.'

'Oh!'

'Yes, for a hen! What do you expect, Sister?... We're not Angels.'"

Awareness of human misery! It was so deeply rooted in our Sister's soul that she gladly brought it up in her conversations. She was asked once if she expected to go straight to Heaven. She answered: "Oh, no… we are so full of imperfections… there is nothing truly good in us. When one sees oneself close to the good God, one is only sin and misery… even what we believe we do well, even the holiest of actions, everything is spoiled by our self-love… No, there is nothing good in us!... It is necessary to humble oneself and leave everything to Our Lord."

"Everything is spoiled by our self-love!" No, self-love spoiled very little in the soul of Sister Mary Martha. However, in the form of "vain complacency," it did try at times to slip itself in.

One day, she rejoiced in the presence of a companion over "a bottle of wine that fell on the stone of the sink not having broken."

Another day, "she says to herself with a certain satisfaction that, for several months, none of the lamps she had filled had yet needed refilling."

And yet another time, having witnessed some damage caused by a neighbor, she vainly considered how she had been more careful.

However, each time, an interior movement of the soul incited a deep regret, along with a resurgence of humility. Our Lord knew, moreover, how to punish these imperfections and bring them to an end for her: "Recognize now what you are of yourself and report everything to your Superior."

Ought we to recount an incident where we encounter Sister Mary Martha's naive familiarity? In 1878, caterpillars had invaded the currant bushes in the garden. The harvest seemed to be lost. But the prayers made by our Sister on July 2, by order of our Very Honorable Mother, were graciously heard.

On the twenty-seventh of the same month, while visiting the infirmary, she thought she could entertain a sick person by recounting "this event"! Was there some vainglory in this? We have to assume so, for the Savior reprimanded her: "How proud you are! I know how to show you what you are of yourself!"

"Good Master, what are You going to do? Are You going to put back the caterpillars?"

Did the Good Master "put back the caterpillars"? We do not know, but two days later the currant bushes were all covered with them. And Jesus articulated for Sister Mary Martha this hard lesson: "My daughter, should all the fruit perish, it would be nothing; what is something is to have shown you your fault…"

How true it is that Our Lord, watching over the soul of His Bride, wanted to instill her with humility! Humility is priceless in the penetrating eyes of the Savior—the other virtues are but false virtues if humility is not placed at the foundation. All of God's graces are lost wherever humility is lacking to ensure their safety. According to the teaching of St. Francis de Sales, Our Lord goes so far as to "chance" our losing all virtues, provided we preserve humility.

We shall conclude this chapter by giving the account of a favor which left an indelible mark on our Sister.

In the midst of a familiar conversation with the Divine Master, Sister Mary Martha's soul suddenly found itself transported to Heaven. She ascended, getting ever closer to the Beloved… And the Blessed, making a select space for her in their ranks, sang in unison with a ravishing voice. They said: "The one who was the littlest becomes the greatest!"

What she understood most clearly at that time was the reality and profoundness of her nothingness. She saw herself as little... little and stripped of everything, having absolutely nothing... But her heart overflowed with immense gratitude to the great God, so good to her little nothingness.

This grace left her with the most insatiable desire to humble herself still more, for she understood more than ever that it was absolutely necessary to humble oneself to reach that place up above!

"And he hath exalted the humble!"

Dear Sister Mary Martha, your desire for a lowly and hidden life was fully answered. You spent your time here below unknown, overlooked, and perhaps at times scorned. From up above, obtain for your younger Sisters that same humility that is irresistible to the Heart of God... and to the gates of Heaven!

## CHAPTER 19

## SPIRIT OF MORTIFICATION AND PENANCE

"𝔜OU are dead to the world and to yourself, for to live no longer but in God," the Visitation Sister is told on the day of her profession. This work of mortification, alluded to in the powerful expression from the Ceremonial, is not accomplished in a single day... It is a long, unending work, always to be continued.

From the first years of her religious career, Sister Mary Martha undertook it with generosity, spurred on by Our Lord Who urged her "to choose, in everything and everywhere, the path where there is the most mortification." To the interior and hidden abnegation that the practice of the evangelical counsels presupposed, and to the many acts of self-denial which constant fidelity to the Rule demanded, she joined, to a rare degree, exterior mortification. Never did she appear to relent in exercising a holy strictness on herself.

In the refectory, she indifferently ate, according to the counsel of the Apostle, "what was set before" her, and, if she was given a choice, she always arranged things so that others were left with the best.

She generally had a very good appetite. Thus, a reduction in what she ate must have been painful for her. However, Jesus asked her at times to give up a portion of her servings. "Because I am poor," He told her.

Like most people, she would have appreciated, on occasion, a taste of something more delicate; but it was precisely on this that the Divine Poor One set His sights... And He had such compelling arguments to convince His Servant, with such touching appeals to move her heart! Let us read the manuscript: "Our sweet Savior appeared to her one day crucified and having been given vinegar and gall to drink. This vision pierced Sister Mary Martha's soul with such heartrending sorrow that the memory of it never left her. 'It is necessary, My daughter,' her good Master told her, 'that you quench My thirst through your mortification. You must make reparation for so many crude faults that are committed in drinking and eating.'"

It was especially during the days when the world gives itself over to pleasures and disorder that Jesus wanted to see reparation from His Chosen One. In 1868, He warned her to prepare for a redoubling of expiatory sufferings in order to make reparation for the sins of intemperance committed during the time of Carnival.

Beginning on that day, anything that the Servant of God tried to eat towards evening, even a little bit of simple soup, caused her terrible pain. This was the prelude to the "great fast" that was soon to be demanded of her and of which we have spoken elsewhere.

However, despite the weakness brought about by the privation of food, Our Lord wanted her to persist firmly in her work. He helped her visibly and invisibly in such a real way that it sufficed for everything.

This steadfastness in her work, despite all kinds of sufferings, was a mark of virtue that we can classify as heroic, and this heroism did not fail for a single day of the rest of her life.

It was especially in the domain of afflictive penances that her courage inspired admiration. Without a doubt, she was not exempt from ordinary sensitivities. Very sensitive she was! Keenly did she feel corporal sufferings... suffering is so contrary to nature! But she knew so well how to give to Jesus! And Jesus knew so well that He could ask anything!

To suffer as Jesus and with Jesus! This was always, for the Privileged One of His Heart, a powerful incentive to penance. This genuine union with the Master's Passion dated back to the first years of her religious life.

A light from on high had given her, at that time, such a profound knowledge of her defects that she felt she was the most miserable creature in the world. As she was humbling herself, immersing herself in the abyss of her own nothingness, Our Lord, granting her a striking vision of His Passion, ordered her to ask permission to take the discipline four times on Fridays in order to unite herself to His divine sufferings.

The permission was requested and obtained. And our Sister executed the discipline with such courage that she shed blood each time.

Shortly afterwards, Jesus invited her to add another one every Thursday (if the Superiors consented) without omitting the ones on Mondays and Wednesdays, "to honor His scourging": "The lashes of the scourging glorify Me because they are shown as an example to My children."

We remember that in 1866, He Himself had taught His Servant to weave herself a crown of thorns. A few years later, He demanded even more: "Your crown no longer makes you suffer enough," He said to her one day. "Go find your Mistress. She has a replacement for it that is appropriate for your head."

The generous novice went in complete simplicity to relay to our Very Honorable Sister Marie-Alexis Blanc the order she had just received. The latter first responded: "No, I don't have anything." Then, after some reflection, she added: "We do have an iron belt, but that can't go on your head... but let's go and see."

Sister Mary Martha tried on the belt. It fit well. The instrument of penance went around her head just like a crown—one would have thought that her measurement had been taken.

This belt or crown, which was fitted with iron spikes, was very painful for her... Sister Mary Martha was tempted to leave the crown aside. But Jesus Christ appeared to her on the Cross suffering horribly, His forehead pierced by the cruel thorns, and large tears falling from His divine eyes... and the redeeming Blood issuing from all the wounds of His Sacred Head: "My daughter, I do not take off My crown," the Savior said to her, as a loving reproach. Upon hearing these words, our Sister became quite ashamed; she courageously put her crown back on and, from then on, no longer hesitated.

The rough hair shirt this dear victim wore day and night, by order of Our Lord, an order that was sanctioned by obedience, also made her suffer horribly. She was about to take it off one day. To encourage her, her good Master said to her: "My daughter, I give you this suffering to win My love." Then, showing her His adorable Wounds, He said: "See, My daughter, how much I have suffered for you!... Could you ever suffer too much for Me?"

There was yet another time when she was about to succumb to the temptation to remove it, so much was the feel of it painful for her, when Jesus stopped her with these words: "I want to have you suffer proportionally to My being offended... You must remember that you are My Bride and My plaything of love." Then, having her taste the delights of Heaven for a few moments, He added: "Is the pain of suffering not worth meriting such happiness? But you must first be, as I was, all torn apart by your hair shirt."

In 1881, the Very Honorable Mother Thérèse-Eugénie Revel gave this testimony regarding Sister Mary Martha: "It has been more than thirteen years now that she spends her nights before the Most Blessed Sacrament or stretched out on the floor of her cell with her instruments of penance: a crown, an iron bracelet, and a hair shirt, except for sometimes when she is very ill, and for two to three weeks during the great freezes of winter, when we require her to put herself in bed."

In all of this, our Sister obeyed the express will of the Master of her soul.

One evening when she was feeling very tired, Sister Mary Martha would have liked to have spent the night in her bed. We told her: "Very well, ask Our Lord permission to take your rest in bed in union with the rest He took in His crib."

Jesus permitted it. But hardly had an hour gone by when He called out to His Servant and said to her: "Although your request honored My Holy Infancy, it is not here that you should remain, My daughter." And Sister Mary Martha had to get up to obey the divine voice.

"She sometimes suffers much; at other times, her heart is united to Jesus Crucified in such an intimate manner that she no longer feels the corporal sufferings, so much is her soul inundated with consolation.

"It is remarkable that after nights of extreme pain, she is strong and energetic the next day like someone who has rested perfectly" (Manuscript).

The Savior, moreover, sometimes rewarded the generosity of His faithful bride by not allowing her to remain without relief.

On January 13, 1869, our dear Sister had just put herself in bed when Our Lord expressed to her the desire to see her spend the night on the floor. She got up unhesitatingly. She did not, however, feel the truly extreme cold of that night; it seemed to her, on the contrary, that she had a furnace on each side of her to warm her.

Our Holy Founders also made parental visits to their humble and heroic daughter. With her customary simplicity, she was once bold enough to ask St. Francis de Sales if the nights spent on the floor were pleasing to him. "Yes," he answered, "because it is the path that God has chosen for you, but it cannot be commanded... It is God Who asks it, and of whom it pleases Him."

## CHAPTER 20

## SISTER MARY MARTHA AND
## THE RELIGIOUS LIFE

IT has been said of the religious vocation that if it is given to the called soul to appreciate already here below, to a certain extent, the grace it has been granted, it is only in eternity that it will comprehend its value.

To be taken from the crowd and set aside for direct and undivided service to the Divine Majesty, to be "wed" to the Son of God, and to be called to cooperate in a special way in the salvation of souls, is a blessing that surpasses all human plans and ambitions, and the thought of which unceasingly inundates the heart with an indelible gratitude.

Of this blessing, Sister Mary Martha Chambon had an awareness that was as keen as it was profoundly supernatural.

She loved her vocation. "She valued it above everything," noted the Superior, after recalling certain temptations from the devil suggesting to our Sister that she would be better off working out her salvation in the world.

Thus, how joyful it was for Sister Mary Martha to hear the Master say to her: "You know why I have chosen you. It is because of your misery, My daughter. It is for My glory and the salvation of souls... My daughter, I want you to thank Me for your call to the religious life on behalf of so many consecrated souls who do not think to do so." And what fervor she exercised

177

in giving herself unreservedly to all of the Divine Bridegroom's intentions!

It was at the time of the annual retreats that our dear Sister especially enjoyed the blessing of her vocation. This time brought her incomparable delights and benefits. Our Lord loved to make Himself her "book" and the Guide of her soul: "You have the treasury of books, for you have Myself. I only need your heart and you do not need any books other than Mine—you will open your heart, you will make yourself very little, and I Myself shall pour in.

"Desiring a book to find Me is wasting your time. You must, My daughter, keep yourself close to Me, forgetting everything to gaze upon Me in your heart. Thus, united to Me in recollection, My love will penetrate you, making you more silent, meeker with your neighbor… and by this means, you will live a heavenly life."

"Oh, Sister, it is in this that I am a gourmand!" added the pious child.

The interior joy experienced during these blessed days showed itself on her exterior. More than one of her solitaire companions remembered that face, at once both recollected and ablaze, which she brought to recreation each evening when the retreatants reunited.

And what to say of the Holy Renewals that came to crown the work of the Retreats? The feast of the Presentation was, without question, one of the dearest and sweetest feasts for her soul. It never passed by without imparting to her a delightful fervor, imbued however with a respectful apprehension due to the grandeur of the day's ceremony—a ceremony that St. Francis de Sales had made especially moving and expressive. One by one, each of the Visitation sisters pronounces the formula that reiterates her consecration to the Bridegroom of Virgins. And immediately the priest, holding a ciborium in his hands, responds by presenting the Sacred Host to her: "May the Body of Our Lord Jesus Christ preserve your soul unto life everlasting!..."

On November 21, 1880, as Sister Mary Martha remained breathless in the middle of the words of the Renewal, the Savior, full of kindness, said to her: "My daughter, I wait for you!... I prefer your heart even more than your words."

On the same day in 1873, Our Lord showed His Beloved the bride-souls approaching the Bridegroom... All were in His Heart, some of them quite deeply immersed inside, others less so... And Jesus said: "*Memoria in aeternum!*"

Surprised, the unlearned child asked: "Good Master, what does that mean?... I do not understand these words."

"My daughter," Jesus answered with tenderness, "this act will be eternal."

The blessed Privileged One then saw the Divine Master uniting to Himself the soul of each Bride with a wondrously beautiful chain of the purest gold. A ring was added to this chain. At the same time, she received such vivid lights concerning the value of the religious vows and the worth of each renewal that her fervent longing for Heaven gave way for a moment to that of living to accomplish many more equally meritorious actions.

\*\*\*

Sister Mary Martha's love for her vocation was continuously nourished by her supernatural relations with the Saints of the Visitation family.

Among the consolations of a religious soul, there is one that is particularly sweet: that of living in intimacy with the Holy Founders of the Institute. These glorious Saints—who simply remain for other persons, even the most fervent, friends or powerful patrons—are, for her, a Father and a Mother in the most real sense of the word: they have given her the life she enjoys in God. Feeding on their writings, by which they continue to speak, is a most cherished duty. She approaches very closely these saints who are venerated at a distance by ordinary persons. She sees them as much on earth as in Heaven. They seem to be present at her side, lending themselves to a delightful familiarity while simultaneously offering themselves for imitation.

This was indeed the case for Sister Mary Martha. She lived in habitual contact and astonishing intimacy with our Holy Founders, confiding to them all of her needs, presenting them her requests, and receiving from them advice and encouragement, accompanied by marks of tenderness that ravished her soul.

St. Francis de Sales, among others, was pleased to converse with his humble daughter. How many times, in the course of our pages, has one been able to catch echoes of these simple conversations between Father and child that call to mind the talks at La Galerie.

"Good-bye, my daughter, I love you much," he concluded one day. "As for you, you see me. Your Sisters do not see me, but I watch them in all their actions… Your Holy Mother and your Sisters are here also, very close."

On the evening of December 28, 1868, while we were venerating the relics of our Holy Father and Doctor following benediction of the Most Blessed Sacrament, he again said to

Sister Mary Martha: "I am here. I give a kiss of love and a grace to each one of my Daughters."

St. Jane Frances de Chantal, for her part, often favored Sister Mary Martha with her maternal visits, giving her advice for her personal instruction or precious messages for our Mothers.

As for St. Margaret Mary, the great lover of the Sacred Heart, she undoubtedly recognized in our humble Mary Martha a younger little Sister whose path, often rough, was not without similarity to her own. She therefore came to bring her help and encouragement in difficult moments.

She reminded her of suffering's worth: "If you knew the value of suffering, you would be unable to stop yourself from desiring it."

She spurred her on in the conquest for souls. She inflamed her with love for Jesus in the Most Blessed Sacrament. On one seventeenth of October, at the moment when our Sister was receiving communion, she whispered: "You are receiving all of your Treasure. It is necessary to love Our Lord so much!"

From this contact and intimacy, there resulted in the soul of Sister Mary Martha not only an admirable intensity in religious life, but also a perpetual renewal of commitment to the Institute where God had marked out a place for her.

There were multiple times, in fact, when St. Francis de Sales' counsels were intended for a more general audience. Through the blessed Privileged One, they were reaching all of the Visitation Sisters. She might then have felt as a very little member of an immense Family to whom the common Father was addressing a Founder's "watchword."

"My daughters, you must go through all of your domain, which is the Holy Rule... I went through much trouble to compose your holy Writings, going into the smallest details. It is today my greatest glory.

"The first of your observances is to study Jesus, not only in prayer, but in everything and everywhere—in work time as in your moments of free time.

"The task of the Visitation Sister on earth is the life of Our Lord at Nazareth. A life of simplicity and of holy childhood: Jesus's infancy... Your actions must be ordinary in the eyes of creatures, but extraordinary to Heaven by means of love.

"I have left my Order an abundant food; it is up to the fidelity of each one to feed herself with it.

"Blessed will they be who do violence to themselves to observe well their rules—they shall be my crown of glory!... My cloak of honor is meekness and humility—by these marks, I recognize my true daughters."

Our Lord Himself seemed to have made it His task to remind her unceasingly, in multiple ways, of the Holy Founder's teachings. In the school of the Divine Master, Sister Mary Martha better understood her personal mission, which was to pray and suffer for all—which was also to help far-off souls destined to enter the Salesian fold. These souls one day seemed to her as sheep in danger, for lack of a bridge, of going over a dangerous precipice: "I confide them to you," said the Sovereign Shepherd, "you will push them towards Me as if you were their shepherdess. These sheep are souls I have chosen for Myself. To draw them to Me, you must keep your heart pressed closely against Mine."

She better understood the necessity—for every Religious—to have a very supernatural spirit and a perfect fidelity to the Rule: "Your life is not of this world," Jesus taught her, "it is the life of Heaven on earth. Since you are not of this world, you must not do the things of this world.

"My Brides are like My Saints… My Brides must be in Heaven in spirit while they work for Me on earth. When you perform an action, an act of observance, the Heavenly Court is watching you."

Shortly after her profession, even before a series of exceptional graces were given her, our dear Sister had received a very penetrating vision of the beauty of our holy Rules and of the blessings attached to their observance. And since then, what divine lessons have been added to this!

One day Our Lord put the entire world before her eyes. He showed her religious, priests, bishops, etc., and in each state there was a different measure of grace. "I shall ask of each one according to what he has received," He said. "But for you, I shall ask one thing only, and that is whether you obeyed well.

"Your path is your Rules and Constitutions. It is a path that will lead you straight to the Visitation in Heaven.

"You do not know in detail the perfection contained in your Holy Rule. If you are faithful to its practice in everything, in the most perfect manner, you will always have new lights to understand it. Each act of observance obtains for you a new light that each act of neglect has you lose, for observance to the Rule gives understanding of the things of Heaven."

She better understood the very spirit of the Visitation: "My daughter," the Savior told her, "ask My Father, for all of the Visitation Sisters, union with Jesus in the hidden life."

On July 2, 1870, all of the Visitation in Heaven appeared to the humble Servant of God as a numerous and triumphant army. This legion of blessed souls stood before Our Lord Jesus Christ, contemplating His glorious Wounds: "They are very close to Me," Jesus said, "because they were very hidden on earth."

"All the glory of your holy Order is for Heaven!" This was to show the eternal joys, but also the road that leads us to them.

This reminder of the hidden life that must be that of the Visitation Sister was again made heard by Our Lord to Sister Mary Martha a few months later:

"During the night of December 13, 1870, He showed her a magnificent banner, in which maxims were etched in golden letters and adorned with precious stones. Jesus had the first three lines read to His Servant. They were but a single word: Union! Union! Union!!!

This word called to mind the desire of our Holy Founders. They wanted us to live in a great union of heart, for "therein is the practice of the spirit of your Holy Order."

But the bottom of the banner surpassed the rest in splendor. This, it was explained to our Sister, was a symbol to show that if the souls who do great things for God are magnificently rewarded in Heaven, more beautiful still will be the crown of those who have lived hidden in humility.

## CHAPTER 21

## CHASTITY

A great preoccupation of Sister Mary Martha, especially during her retreats, was often that of finding matter of which to accuse herself in the Holy Tribunal. In the candor of her perfect simplicity, she believed she did not know how to make a proper confession! What to do, if not implore the Sovereign Master of her soul…

"My Jesus, I would really like to know how to confess like our Sisters."

"My daughter, each one has her conscience and it is not necessary to conform oneself to others," Our Lord answered. "The faults of some are not those of others. You yourself have no more knowledge of evil than a little child who does not yet have reason."

The good Master repeated this last expression to His chosen one multiple times.

"We believe with certainty," wrote the personal confidante of all of Sister Mary Martha's struggles, and of the Savior's graces towards her, "we believe with certainty that her soul preserved intact the robe of Baptism. One day, seeing her anxious about confession, her conscience not reproaching her for anything in particular, we said to her: 'You must accuse yourself of one of your life's greatest sins.' She answered: 'I do not know what they are, Mother. Perhaps some little acts of disobedience to my parents?'" (Very Honorable Mother Thérèse-Eugénie).

Our Sister's childhood, in fact, was spent in the religious calm of the fields and under the vigilance of a maternal eye. And Our Lord Himself made sure to keep from her anything that might deflower this virginal purity.

The villagers of La Croix-Rouge often went down to Chambéry to sell fruit from their gardens or the excellent products from their farms. One day some girls were going to the market, and Madame Chambon entrusted Françoise to them. What danger did she run into? We do not know exactly, but an instinctive fright suddenly took hold of her, and guided, she believed, by St. Joseph, the poor child ran back home. And her mother, seeing her trembling, decided against ever sending her into the city again.

Entering the monastery with a blessed ignorance of evil, Sister Mary Martha remained a truly angelic soul. Thus, in this chapter titled "Chastity," it is really a matter of crystal-clear innocence and virginal love.

"My Beloved delights among the lilies," says the chaste Bride in the Canticles. Jesus, the Lily of the Valley, takes His delight in the virginal soul, in which He finds a reflection of His divine purity…

"Blessed are the pure in heart, for they shall see God… My daughter, pure hearts, I unite them to Mine!… Your souls and your bodies were formed by My hand, they must be much respected—they shall glory together before Me."

The Angels, forming the guard of honor around the Tabernacle, also made her to understand how our fragile flesh was a cause of greater glory to God when consecrated to His love.

The Blessed Virgin came to complete the teachings and invitations. On one feast of the Visitation (in 1875), she appeared accompanied by our Sisters in Heaven: "I show them to you," she said to her child of predilection, "see how they are happy in my train... One day, you shall be here also... Our Lord wants everything in His brides to be pure, chaste, and holy... It is necessary to occupy one's mind with the things of Heaven... You must present Jesus a heart that is empty so that He can fill it."

### *Virginal Love*

A chaste heart, Blessed Adeodatus says, is one which loves God alone: "*Ille est vere castus qui ad Deum attendit et ad ipsum solum se tenet.*"

"One day," writes our Holy Mother de Chantal, "Our Lord made known to me after Holy Communion that if a soul wants to keep itself interiorly and exteriorly for Him, it has only to put into practice the *Constitution on Chastity*.[1] He told me, 'Its words are entirely divine, there is nothing human in them, everything came from My loving heart.'"

---

[1] "There is no need to state how much the Sisters are obligated in this, for, in short, they must live, breathe, and take in air only for their heavenly Bridegroom, in all honesty, purity, cleanness, and holiness of spirit, in words, deportment, and actions, by immaculate and angelic conversation" (St. Francis de Sales, *Constitution on Chastity*).

It is necessary to read the conferences on simplicity and modesty to understand how far our holy Doctor extends the powers of perfect chastity. They are almost confused with the effects of perfect love since this chastity must produce unity in the thoughts as well as in the affections (Preface to St. Francis de Sales' *Conferences* [edition unspecified]).

Let us now listen to the unlettered Sister Mary Martha:

"One day, desirous of penetrating further into the secret of the Bridegroom," her spiritual helper recounted, "I tactfully tried to probe her: 'You know, my good Sister Mary Martha, our Holy Founder wants us to charitably communicate our little blessings with each other. Speak to me then about your childhood, and about God's mercies towards you... The remembrance of these things does so much good, does it not?'

"'Oh, yes! He is all love, the good God! When I was a very little girl, He already then allowed me to sense Him. He spoiled me so much! I know nothing of the world, I know only Him! Oh, how I love Him!'

"'But why then does Our Lord love you so much? What is there in you that attracts Him?'

"And she answered me with delightful candor: 'Oh, Sister, it is because I am ignorant, I have a heart that is simple and without lining... also, I have a heart that is detached—He Himself is everything!... I hold on to nothing, to nothing... I need nothing, I desire nothing; my heart is free.'

"All of this, I sensed, was profoundly true. 'However,' I responded, 'your job, you seem to like it and take interest in it?'

"'The garden? Yes, because it is obedience.'

"'And your nephews? Don't they have a little place in your heart? Do you think about them sometimes?'

"'My nephews? Oh, not much. I ask God that they remain good Christians; other than that, I never think about them. One does not have the time to think about so many things, one is so happy with our little Jesus!... He is quite enough, don't you think, Sister Assistant?'"

Do not the purity and detachment of this soul manifest themselves so clearly?

During thanksgiving after a fervent communion, Sister Mary Martha heard Jesus exhort her further in this perfect detachment: "You, my bride, you must go high! He Whom you receive is not here—look at Him..." She saw Our Lord in an immense light. He continued: "I want your affections to be high up, well above the earth."

Love is the gift of self. To love exclusively, to give oneself without holding anything back for oneself is the virginity of love.

Jesus calls for this virginity of love in the hearts of His Brides.

"Being a religious, My daughter, is to have banished from one's heart all created things... It is to everywhere see only Jesus, your Bridegroom, it is to seek Him exclusively. The Bride who does not do this will expose herself to much suffering... She will gain little and often be troubled."

One day, while the Community was gathered together for the "Obedience," the Divine Master suddenly appeared above the place of the Superior, and addressing everyone in the person of the blessed child, who alone had the privilege of seeing and hearing Him, He said: "You are all standing,[2] what is it you desire? Your goal must be to be with Me one-on-one. All of you know this. But some are too attached to temporal things. They do not think that I alone must be their Everything.

---

[2] At the signal given by the bell, all the Sisters line up around the meeting room and remain standing as they await orders from the Superior.

"When I am sought fervently, I come to the soul that desires Me. You can shorten the time of trial through a greater hunger for Me."

This is a point Jesus very often repeats: "There is no Bridegroom like Myself. I am thinking constantly about you... Love Me always!... I Myself am always loving you! Your Bridegroom's love is eternal!

"Be thankful... Lose yourself in love for Me, breathe only for Me... Just as I belong entirely to each one, I want to be alone in your affections."

"You are everything to Me! I must also be your Everything!... It is a great thing to be God's everything!

"You must rise up above yourselves to be one-on-one with Me. I want you for Myself alone... I do not want there to be a fiber in your hearts that is not entirely Mine! I want you to be without desires... I want the earth to be nothing to you, nothing."

In the efficacious anointing of these words, Sister Mary Martha felt her heart leap in her breast: "Oh!" she exclaimed, seized with love, "Oh, my beloved Jesus, I give You my heart and the hearts of my Mothers... and those of our Sisters... and of all creatures, even of those who do not love You!"

Hearts that did not love Him Whom she loved so much! At this thought, her own heart was pierced with sorrow: "Oh, my Jesus, how is it that You have created these hearts and they do not love You?... They do not know how good You are!"

"Behold the flames I give to My brides," replied the good Master. "I accept your offering. My beloved, offer Me often your heart and those of all My creatures."

Sister Mary Martha's detachment, as perfect as it was, sometimes succumbed to slight weaknesses.

During one of those delightful days when Our Lord provided her continuous and sensible company, the blessed Privileged One was nevertheless going, out of caprice, to speak a word to her Mistress. The Heavenly Bridegroom's jealousy was thereby excited. He stopped her with this loving reproach: "Am I not enough for you? You must carry on performing your actions in My presence…"

"I want your hearts in their entirety, in order to make up for the ingratitude of men."

Another day, as our Sister's thoughts were dwelling somewhat on her family's temporal affairs, her Divine Master said to her: "What is this, My daughter, you are thinking on the good of your parents and you are neglecting My own."

It is in this way that Our Lord "is jealous of the hearts of His brides."

But Jesus does not leave unrewarded the spirit of sacrifice and true detachment of the heart. It had been a long time that Sister Mary Martha had gone without praying for her parents and she was anxious because of this: "My Jesus," she said to her customary Refuge, "I am remiss in my duty, I forget my parents."

"And I," answered the Savior with tenderness, "I think on them every day. Just as I shall give the religious soul the hundredfold I have promised, in the same way shall I give it to your parents."

# CHAPTER 22

## OBEDIENCE

"𝕴T is obedience that makes the Religious," declares our Holy Mother Jane Frances de Chantal.

One can, in fact, preserve virginity in the world; one can practice poverty there by keeping one's heart detached, even amidst riches. That is relatively easy. However, through the vow of obedience, the human soul sacrifices what it is most averse to giving up, what God has placed in it that is more personal, more noble, and more exalted: judgment and free will. Yes, this freedom of willing and acting is the too dear Isaac that the Religious must sacrifice to God, entirely and forever! The vow of obedience is an essential and distinctive fundamental of the life she has embraced.

Divinely instructed and generously docile, Sister Mary Martha was an obedient soul.

In a spirit of profound faith, she truly recognized God in authority.

Authority, that is to say the Word again made incarnate, not sacramentally under the species of bread, but morally under human appearances to further sustain our souls with the divine word.

"He who hears you, hears Me; he who despises you, despises Me." Is this not the Savior's unchanging, twenty-centuries-old teaching? Undoubtedly, it pertains here to the power to teach that is given to the Church; however, it is also necessary to see in this the share of authority God delegates to His representatives.

"My daughter, your Superior is I," Jesus often repeated to His bride.

On multiple occasions, at the time of the "Obedience," Jesus appeared in the place of the Superior and as though fused together with her as a single person: "Look," He said, "look... It is I Who am in the place of your Mother... It is I Who listen to what is said to her... She holds My place and I hold hers... Her responses are My own."

Similarly, at the "Chapter," Our Lord sometimes took the place of the Superior or, rather, the person of our Mother disappeared and became Jesus before the ravished eyes of the humble seer.

He came in this way to reassign jobs. Beside Him were our Holy Founders, and Jesus spoke through the mouth of our Mother: "I come," He said on one of these occasions, "because your Mother has need of Me. She desired that I direct everything. She asked Me for this. I come thus to give the work roles and, to each one, the grace to receive well what the obedience will decide. You must not worry, you others—think only of Jesus, tend only to Jesus... and Jesus shall do everything for you."

With such lights illuminating her soul, one can imagine Sister Mary Martha's attitude in approaching her Superiors. It is impossible to conceive of greater humility, respect, and veneration. One sensed that our Sister made herself little and was deeply aware of her own nothingness, as though unworthy to approach God's representative.

One can also imagine how trustingly she surrendered herself to their guidance, and how much weight their least decisions had for her. The very thought, "Our Mother told me," cut short any self-initiative. It was also the ever-effective remedy against doubt's assaults and fear's insinuations.

Trust in authority which, united to a childlike simplicity, went so far as to "work miracles"—proof of this fact is recorded in the manuscripts.

"Our little Sister was ill and in bed for a few days. Our Very Honorable Sister Marie-Alexis Blanc, her Directress, went to see her and gave her this word of encouragement: 'Tomorrow you will have recovered.' Sister Mary Martha understood this literally... and such great faith ravished the Heart of Jesus. He gave her perfect health at that very moment and said: 'As proof of your recovery, I want you to take your meal this evening as if you were with your Sisters in the refectory.' It truly required confidence and a spirit of faith on our part to serve the normal Community meal to a sick person who had only drunk water for several days. She ate everything that was served to her.[1] She slept very peacefully that night, rose the next day for Mass, and went back to her job and ordinary duties" (Manuscript).

This perfect trust in the Superior's authority was precisely one of the things in which the devil tried to trouble our Sister. Through deceitful insinuations, he often tried to prevent her from having recourse to those who had the grace to enlighten and support her in her sometimes quite difficult path. It happened that, for a few days, Sister Mary Martha experienced an extreme repugnance to approaching our Very Honorable Mother. As she was placing this difficulty before the feet of

---

[1] Without drinking, our Very Honorable Mother added parenthetically, attributing it to Sister Mary Martha's mortification—the infirmarian had forgotten to give her a drink.

Jesus one evening, she heard His voice: "Look, My daughter, at this lamp that enlightens My brides... If you light it each day without adding any oil, what would become of it? It would no longer give its light."

Our Lord, then developing the analogy, made His Servant to understand that trust is to the torch of the Mother as oil is to the lamp—it enables her to provide her light. "If you distance yourself from your Superior, you will go astray and lose true light."

"The Superior is light—it is necessary to have recourse to her."

"Superiors, to be good, must give their children spiritual death—this is their entire task," the Divine Master taught another time. And Sister Mary Martha saw a path open up before her that was completely flooded with light: "To travel this path, your Superiors must have you die to yourselves, to nature. Indocile souls, who do not want to be directed or corrected, do not enter upon it... they travel an obscure and dark path."

Our Sister most certainly followed this luminous path. We know that, furthering the designs of God, her Superiors provided her numerous occasions to die to nature. But whatever she received from their maternal lips, whether rebuke or encouragement, whether an order or a prohibition, never did one witness her stray from total submission or profound humility.

Let us listen to the testimony of her male and female Superiors. They were unanimous in affirming that one could impose on her whatever work and ask of her whatever sacrifice without encountering the least bit of resistance. Never did she protest. Never did she dispute an order that was given.

Such was the affirmation of our holy Chaplains, Canons Bouvier and Collonge, who each directed her conscience for more than twenty years: "She was most obedient," they both stated, "and followed the advice she was given to the letter."

"Obedience is everything to her," we likewise read in the declarations of our Very Honorable Mother Thérèse-Eugénie Revel. Whether orders from her Superiors or commands from God, we saw her obey with true faithfulness.

This was also the testimony of Sister Mary Martha's last Superiors. They recognized that the word "obedience" had an all-powerful effect on her. It alone had the power to take her from her long and profound contemplation at the feet of the Divine Master. As soon as our Mother had spoken, or anyone of us on her behalf, our Sister rose promptly to report to the designated place.[2] Did Our Lord not tell her that "My grace is attached to the promptness of obedience"?

Religious obedience does not only consist in submission to the orders, counsels and immediate desires of Superiors. There are, throughout the day and throughout life, a host of prescriptions established by the Holy Founders and approved by the Church to which the Religious must subject herself to remain faithful to God.

"The truly obedient person," says St. Francis de Sales, "loves his Rules and honors them as the true path of his soul's union with God, and embarking upon it, he never strays from it."[3]

---

[2] A good elder Sister, who was a bit envious—but in a holy way—of the divine favors of her companion, ventured one day to go and shake her, as was sometimes done on behalf of the Superior in order to wake her from her mystical sleep. Sister Mary Martha opened her eyes and gently said, "Do you have permission?"

[3] Conference 11 (on the virtue of obedience).

Sister Mary Martha, as any true Religious, had the spirit of obedience, that is to say the love of obedience vowed to God in the person of her Superiors. She did not have any less love for the Rules and Constitutions, the importance and beauty of which she understood through the supernatural lights she had received.

Several times already has our account touched on our Sister's regret regarding these blessed Rules, that she feared and lamented not observing them well.

One point especially preoccupied her: that of punctuality for the Community's meetings, from which her job close to our students habitually kept her. We know that during vacations she made up for this with an inexpressible consolation. One saw her arrive full of joy with the words of the Psalmist on her lips: "Behold how good and how pleasant it is for brethren to dwell together in unity!"

Other than these exceptions imposed by duty, Sister Mary Martha was very exact in observing everything that she could of our holy prescriptions.

The rule of silence was particularly important to her. Her companions remember with edification how strictly she observed it, especially during Lent.

Concerning religious modesty and gravity, we know she had a deeply recollected bearing, her eyes always lowered when they were not closed.

As for our Spiritual Directory, it was infinitely precious to her and we can say that she practiced it in its perfection, since her orientation towards God was constant.

She never knew how to *read* the words placed at the beginning of this little book, but she *lived* them, and so many times did they surface on her lips as a formula especially dear to her soul.[4]

---

[4] "May all of their life and exercises be for uniting them to God, for helping, through prayer and good example, the Holy Church and the salvation of neighbor; and, for this, they must desire nothing so much as to be so virtuous that their good fragrance, being pleasing to God, spreads into the hearts of the faithful" (Spiritual Directory, art. 1).

# CHAPTER 23

## POVERTY

N O word better expresses the sentiments of our former tertiary of St. Francis of Assisi. Evangelical poverty was truly Sister Mary Martha's favorite virtue and—just like humility—her soul's holy passion.

Certainly, her entrance into the convent was not a great material sacrifice for her—born into a very modest family, she did not have to renounce a fortune or the luxury and comforts that accompany it. For the same reason, certain privations that were so harsh for novices raised in different circumstances did not constitute a major suffering for her. This does not make it less true that she acquired in the cloister the true spirit of poverty and that she practiced this virtue in a heroic manner, to its full extent, and in its most varied forms.

Here, as everywhere else, the examples of Our Lord held the prime place in her formation.

One remembers the lights that came to her in the first years of her religious life concerning the excellence and the beauty of the vow of poverty, through the image of the newborn Jesus: "Never did a child appear to the world in greater poverty," she was told. She saw the Divine Child wrapped in swaddling clothes, having only Mary's arms and the breath of animals to warm Him... O destitution, sufferings, privations, and humiliations of the Savior and His Holy Mother, you are a sermon for His brides.

One day Sister Mary Martha was praying the Stations of the Cross. At the tenth station, Our Lord made her to understand how His being stripped merited graces in favor of the souls called to follow Him in poverty. And He asked her to offer the Holy Wounds "for those of His brides who need to strip themselves, so that they know how to 'reclothe' Him through a more careful practice of their vow of poverty."

Continuing to instruct His faithful disciple, the Divine Crucified One portrayed to her this austere virtue as the sacrificing knife that not only cuts off attachments to exterior and sensible objects but also probes mercilessly into the deepest recesses of the soul to strip it of everything: "It is truly only the souls of religious who can participate fully in My self-divestment on the Cross by letting themselves be stripped by the pain of the present moment in the way God desires."

From Jesus in the tabernacle, there was the same lesson and the same appeal: "Look at Him Who is here, how poor He is!... Conform yourself to this Example. A heart only possesses Me fully when it is completely stripped of itself and of creatures. In this poverty there is the fullness of wealth. In the tabernacle, just as on the Cross, My daughter, I am stripped of everything... I want the soul of the religious to be this way: she must lose her own spirit and take on that of Jesus.

"To conquer My Heart, you must be poor, having only what is necessary. What is superfluous belongs to Me, you must give it to Me."

Sister Mary Martha, it is well presumed, never had anything superfluous and always limited herself to what was strictly necessary.

She was in fact poor in everything. She was so in her worn-out clothing, which was extremely patched up.

She was so in her food, taking for herself, with permission, what others discarded, completely spoiled fruit that she alone could eat.

She was so in her work, "taking extreme care in handling all things, breaking almost nothing in her post as boarding school refectorian, in which the opportunities to do damage were nevertheless frequent. In her hands, the most fragile objects were preserved indefinitely, almost without any deterioration" (Manuscript).

She was so in her good use of time, for this is one of the demands of religious poverty.

Sister Mary Martha was naturally very active and it is remarkable that the most signal graces and the most profound recollection never harmed her work. "She did a lot of work," say all her companions, and there was no one like her for helping someone "get out of a difficulty." "It is clear and proven," declared the Very Honorable Mother Thérèse-Eugénie Revel, "that she daily does the work of two persons."

God, of course, gave her the energy. But He also gave her the understanding of the vow and virtue of poverty with the conviction that she did not have the right to waste one moment of her time.

"My child," Jesus had told her, "you must not waste any time. All your minutes are Mine; if you waste any of them, it is stealing from Me, and from your neighbor... I want you to ask what you are to do with great humility, like a poor woman who is very obliged when someone wants to give her some work... I want you to serve your neighbor, the students as much as the Sisters, without ever refusing work, but rather seeing yourself as very honored that one wants to make use of you."

It was also in the spirit of poverty that the dear Lay Sister so zealously harvested fruits and vegetables, ensuring nothing was wasted. In the spirit of poverty, she gathered one by one the individual grapes that had fallen on the ground during harvest... And we never fail—when the season comes—to call to mind Sister Mary Martha carefully tending to this work. In a spirit of poverty, she joined to the herbs from the garden the wild sorrel found in the meadow... and, in the dead of winter, found a way to still unearth, beneath the snow, fresh vegetables that she brought like a treasure to the Sister Cook.

She understood that the monastery's property is God's property; she cared for it as such and suffered when she perceived some negligence in this respect.

"Sister Mary Martha hardly gave lessons," says one of her companions whose testimony has been cited multiple times. "She was so humble! She only remarked on breaches of poverty."

This great spirit of poverty was not always understood by young Sisters who acted somewhat heedlessly... She was at times accused of avarice and of thinking only of material things.

This was something that affected her and reveals to us what sincere humility accompanied her spirit of poverty—these reproaches often plunged her into great sorrow, for, she said, "It must really be true since my neighbor says so."

Towards the end of her life, she also confided this "thorn" to her spiritual helper: "There are some of our Sisters who say that I am attached to cabbage and spinach... Oh, no! It is only that it pains me when I see things wasted, because they are the good God's blessings. It is He Who gives them to us... And besides, we have taken the vow of poverty!"

Did our dear Sister sometimes take things to extremes? That would, of course, not be surprising. That is why, delicate as we are, we do at times attribute to her an overzealousness in wanting others to share an overly austere poverty! But also, after having smilingly recalled these memories—and realizing that our charitable Sister herself smiles at us from up above—it is very sweet to reread in the manuscripts such consoling words from the Divine Master Who Himself knew the heart of His Servant: "My daughter, they believe you are very avaricious due to the great attention you put into gathering the least bit of fruit and carefully handling everything. I judge you quite differently. I know how much your heart is detached from the things of the earth!" These words are the truth.

Yes, our Sister was poor through this detachment from all created things, through this absolute interior self-divestment... She was truly stripped, truly detached, free of all hindrances, and quite close to that most sublime summit where poverty and chastity unite in a fraternal kiss, in such a way that, poor in everything, the soul is rich in God alone. One will recall the candid response cited earlier: "I have a heart that is detached... He Himself is everything... I hold on to nothing, to nothing, I desire nothing... my heart is free."

# CHAPTER 24

# THE CHARITY OF SISTER MARY MARTHA

## *Her Love for God*

ISTER Mary Martha "held on to nothing." Her heart was "free." It was because the love of God consumed her entirely. Detached from created things, no fetters kept her from soaring.

The appeals of Jesus Crucified, the intimacies of Holy Communion, and the fervent communications of the Holy Ghost had enkindled and maintained a fire of love in her soul. Thus, the wondrous stream of graces of which her life consisted, although entirely gratuitous, encountered in her an admirable cooperation—a cooperation that called for newer graces still. So much so that every day divine charity increased in our Sister in all its forms: the tender and trusting love of a child, the pure and chaste love of a virgin, the exclusive love of a bride, and the fervent and powerful love of a lover at Calvary…

We find in the richest period of her life the marks of these divine assaults that, in a certain way, inflamed her body as much as her soul: "I want My Heart to inflame your own. I need this as do you since I want to communicate Myself to My creatures through you." It seemed afterwards and until her last day that this interior fire preferentially gave forth a prayer of intercession that rose to Heaven like an incense of love—a prayer that expressed all of Sister Mary Martha's soul and satisfied her need to love and make reparation, while also winning for God many conquests. Yet the humble nun remained unknown to herself, so consumed by a love that went so far as to devour her vision of the Savior's ineffable workings in her soul, and of a transformation that culminated in a kind of identification with the Bridegroom.

Her spiritual helper asked her one day: "Sister Mary Martha, it doesn't tire you to remain on your knees all morning on an empty stomach?"

"I don't know, I don't think about those things."

"Certainly, you must be tired afterwards?"

"Oh, no, one loses awareness of where one is."

"You must say a lot to the little Jesus during all of that time?"

"Oh, no… we love each other."

"We love each other!" These words are the supreme expression of the Bridegroom and the Bride! These words, plainly expressed by a simple girl from the fields, constitute the single expectation, the single ambition, and the single triumph of Jesus! "We love each other!" Everything Our Lord asked of Sister Mary Martha—work, prayer, suffering, and apostolate—and everything He gave her—trials or graces—all of these things were but one blossoming of love having but one goal: to nourish, manifest, and prove mutual love… "We love each other!"

This mutual love between the Savior and His chosen bride, we can say that it shows itself in every page of this work, in the teachings of the Master and in the actions of the disciple. And if among Jesus's lessons there are some that are particularly moving, it is those on divine love. Is He not the Master of divine love par excellence?

"Loving is the life of Heaven destined for you," He told His Privileged One. "This life, you must live it now as much as you are able."

"You must live it." This was to make her understand that His Brides have less need for speculative knowledge than those persons destined by their state to direct and teach. For His Brides, the essential thing is the practical science of love through union and good works. "The one thing necessary is to possess God."

"If you want to learn to know Me, I shall teach you," Jesus said to her. "Follow Me everywhere, I alone can instruct you."

And revealing the wound of His Sacred Heart, the good Master added: "Come, My child, come and immerse yourself inside. By surrendering one's heart to God, the soul receives lights and graces to love which no book can give."

"I shall teach you to love Me, for you do not know how. The science of love is given to the soul who gazes at the Divine Crucified One and speaks with Him heart to heart."

"My daughter," continued the Savior, "to find Him Whom you seek, you must enter the recess of your heart—there you can behold Me and I shall behold you. My secret of love is revealed to the soul that unites herself to Me and converses with Me in the depths of her heart."

And what is this secret? The Bridegroom only reveals it to the soul for whom it is reserved. "My daughter, I have thousands of favored souls. I am unique to each one. It is a secret of love that shall remain exclusively between the Bridegroom and the Bride for eternity."

Urged by the Beloved's own desires, Sister Mary Martha asked Him one day that all the Sisters of the Community know how to converse well with Him heart to heart. "Oh," Jesus answered with an expression of ardent tenderness, "how this pleases Me, for it is for Me!... Those who converse with Me in their heart are My delight. In this heart to heart, reparation is made to Me for men's ingratitude."

However bold and confident pure love may be, it nevertheless remains subject here below to the dictates of a holy fear—the dust of the earth can so easily tarnish the most beautiful crystal! The Divine Master reassured His bride.

Jesus was once showing Sister Mary Martha the place destined for her in Heaven. Immediately, she humbled herself interiorly and asked with a certain anxiousness: "Good Master, is there nothing in me that prevents me from going there?"

"There are things," Our Lord sweetly answered, "but love effaces everything."

How many times did Jesus repeat to her this consoling phrase that expresses so well the action of perfect contrition in souls: "Love effaces everything."

One day, feeling a strong desire to be united to Him, our Sister beseeched the Savior to take her to Heaven. Jesus seemed not to listen to her... She then cried out: "Oh, my Jesus, here one always runs the risk of offending you!"

"My daughter, love effaces everything."

And when, with insistence, she further asked her good Master to at least grant her the grace to never offend Him again, He answered: "When you come to Me with love, I do not look at your faults, I only look at your love... Love effaces everything."

Another day Sister Mary Martha did not dare approach the Holy Table, being mindful of some infidelity. Our Lord reassured her with these identical words: "Love purifies everything."

"Good Master, is it only today that I shall be purified?"

"No, my daughter, the soul is purified every time that it loves with a strong love. But it must be a true love, pure and detached from everything.

"The Bride who loves can act freely. I see to the purification of her soul to the extent that she labors in my love.

"My union with you is your only good—therein lies your advancement, and no one can prevent it.

"You must be like a thorn on the branch to which it is attached."

We know how much the dear Lay Sister advanced in this blessed union.

Sister Mary Martha was making her Stations of the Cross. Arriving at the fifth and sixth stations, she saw bruised and bloody arms place themselves next to her own outstretched arms. And Jesus said to her: "Behold, My daughter, how My arms are your arms."

This was to express to her in a sensible way the union to which, in so many forms, He invited her: "I only need your heart," He loved to repeat. And showing her His open Heart: "You only need Mine."

"Rest upon My Heart. The Bride's place is upon the Heart of her Bridegroom. You are here for time and for eternity."

When unifying love thus fills a soul, all pusillanimity vanishes from it. And this was—one ever more understands it—the secret of Sister Mary Martha's heroic generosity. Despite all of the kindness, tenderness, and ineffable condescension the Divine Master showed in His dealings with her, it pleased Him to subject her to states of extreme suffering. The demands sometimes reached a level that unsettles us. And these demands, first addressed to a young religious of twenty-five years of age, would mark out, with more or less intensity, her entire existence. In 1887, the Very Honorable Mother Thérèse-Eugénie Revel would again note: "Our Lord continually tells His faithful spouse: 'My daughter, climb Calvary with Me.' Despite her usual great sufferings, He wanted her to keep going without asking for rest." One day He declared to her forcefully: "I want you to be a standing victim!"

… *Standing*, thanks to the strength divine charity provided.

### Charity Towards Neighbors

"Divine charity, entering into a heart, draws after it the entire train of virtues," writes the holy Bishop of Geneva.

Among them all, the love for neighbor is the infallible mark of the love the creature bears for God: "One shall recognize you as My disciples if you love one another as I have loved you."

Sister Mary Martha loved God supremely. This love reflected onto creatures in the form of fraternal charity and complete dedication. One can say that, under Jesus's direction and in union with Him, she gave her neighbor her time, her heart, and her life.

However, it must be said that, here also, her virtue sometimes remained veiled to the benefit of humility.

Our Sister did not possess certain advantages that naturally attract sympathy, the lack of which, for our human sensibilities, doubles the cost of the least services, attentions, and kindnesses. God had not given her beauty of face, gaze, or voice, no more than grace or elegance in bearing and gestures. Her interactions in this respect were deprived of agreeableness, and her charity, which did not express itself as well in external demonstrations, was not always recognized for its true worth.

Furthermore, her multiple occupations led her from time to time to request help from one or another of her companions who was already sufficiently busy. And one saw in this that she at times lacked discretion and appropriateness. She was reproached for it. She incidentally had a response—her response—for everything.

"But why then, Sister Mary Martha," a Sister asked, "why are you constantly asking help from others? Don't you understand that it's annoying when one is overtasked?"

"Sister, it is necessary to teach the young ones to sacrifice themselves… Charity! There is nothing greater, you see."

Her interlocutor said nothing. She believed there was another reason: She thought Sister Mary Martha, smitten with mortification and humiliation, acted thus to earn a rebuke. We tend to think she was right. It seems Our Lord was pleased at times, so as to humble His Bride, to have her seek out help needlessly. Admission of this escaped our Sister one day. She had gone to the fruit loft to request help from a companion to carry a brazier to the refectory. The latter Sister, who was in a hurry to get some work done, could not refrain from replying, "Oh, my poor Sister, instead of coming here, couldn't you have just more quickly carried it by yourself?"

"That's true, Sister, but He wants it like this."

"But how is it you always know where we are?" the workers asked, not without some impatience.

"It's my good Angel who led me," she simply replied.

As for the help to perform, it was always very short, she was not taking advantage of others… After two or three minutes, she sent the Sister away, assuring her that she could finish alone.

Let us hasten to add, moreover, that she herself willingly came to the help of her neighbor. Our Lord had specifically asked her to practice this charity: "Never consider yourself… never refuse a service."

This was so well known that one of our Sister cooks, who had a mischievous psychology, had found an unfailing way to keep the helpers Sister Mary Martha would come to take from her. Seeing Sister Mary Martha running up to a postulant or novice saying, "Young one, come quickly to help me, I am behind schedule," she would object, "Oh, Sister, if you only knew how much of a hurry we ourselves are in, Your Charity would give us a hand." Immediately our Sister would sit down without saying a word, peel the vegetables and dehull the beans, and there was no further mention of her own work. The trick was always successful. Always successful because Sister Mary Martha's good heart and her love for God did not permit her to refuse a service to her neighbor.

And when her customary labor afforded her a break, we already know how willingly she put herself at the service of others. During the boarding school vacations, a Sister who was not that strong and in charge of the cellar saw the charitable Lay Sister warmly wait for her each day fifteen minutes prior to meals to transport the bottles to the community refectory.

This kindness was but one of the forms of charity she drew from the Heart of Jesus and which was, therefore, profoundly supernatural.

"I am all Charity and it is I Who am at work in the one who practices charity. Those who are Mine must have great charity towards their neighbors… a love without limit, but a love that is supernatural and detached."

Supernaturally, Sister Mary Martha did not show preference for anyone in particular. She loved all of her Sisters equally and, following her good Master's recommendation, "carried all of them in her heart."

We have mentioned how much she took interest in each one of us, how much she prayed for each one. She felt continually incited to this: "You must love your neighbor so much," the heavenly voices told her, "and do for her what you would not have the will to do for yourself. Your neighbor must perceive in you a good heart, the Heart of God."

What support she gave to her neighbor! What true kindness, and what compassion for every weakness, every hardship, and every suffering… And how easily did she forget offenses!

"I do not remember," testified one of her companions, "Sister Mary Martha saying a hurtful word to me or hearing her say one to our Sisters. I often refused her minor services. She would return asking me another time with the same simplicity." That was a distinctive feature of her humble charity.

Never did our dear Sister attribute any evil to her neighbor's shortcomings in her regard. If one combs the manuscripts in their entirety, one does not find a single reference to the many little annoyances of which she was the object. One could get away with wronging her, she always blamed herself first.

Jesus one day showed Sister Mary Martha His Head crowned with thorns: "Among My Saints," He told her, "there are some who took part in causing these wounds, yet I love them and treat them as friends...

"My daughter, with your neighbor you must, following My example, have great kindness, forget all offenses, and think only of forgiving and doing new favors. This is the practice of children-souls, in whom I take My delight."

"When, after having lacked humility and patience towards this holy Sister, I asked her forgiveness," further recounted one of her companions, "I sensed that she forgave from the bottom of her heart."

As for her own faults, we have seen[1] how sincerely she made amends for them, and how she thereby always maintained her heart in sweet and peaceful harmony with her companions.

All of this was indicative of—along with a spirit of self-denial and humility—a deep love of neighbor.

A very supernatural love, we have said. But, at the same time, an impulse of a naturally good heart. Thus, beneath her rough exterior, it is not difficult to believe that Sister Mary Martha suffered from her own rusticity. She would have found joy—she who was so deeply loving—in being more lovable and more loved. But the jealous love of her Bridegroom did not permit it. He told her one day at Holy Communion: "Come, My daughter, I want to give you the two virtues of My Heart: meekness and humility. With these, you will make reparation to My adorable Heart! Despite this, I shall allow you from time to time to fall into some fault before your neighbor in order to keep you hidden."

---

[1] Chap. 18 on her humility.

Another time, Jesus made the same promise, accompanied with the same qualification: "I shall grant you the virtues of My meek and humble Heart, yet I for My part shall be directing them… As for you, My daughter, you shall keep your noticeable defects so that you remain hidden and humbled."

Encouraging words for all souls. Concerning the Privileged One with whom we are dealing, do we not know Our Savior's purpose? To protect her from any attacks of pride and to reassure the guides of her soul: "All this must prove to your Superiors that what is transpiring within you comes from God, for of yourself you are very miserable and very imperfect." Very ignorant also, He could have added… And we understand that Jesus had sheltered His "violet" in the shadow of humility and abjection and had surrounded his "lily" with thorns, so that the creature did not approach too closely!

# CHAPTER 25

## APOSTOLIC ZEAL

ONE thing that particularly struck the familiars of Sister Mary Martha and that could not have escaped the reader—given how all of her admirable life was filled with the supernatural—was the apostolic spirit that animated and sustained her.

There was nothing narrow about our Sister's piety. There was nothing egotistical in her prayers. She understood she was a member of the Mystical Body of Jesus Christ, from which she never separated herself.

Her apostolate was not restricted to identifying with her Community and her Institute. She was one with the entire Church.

In investing her with a mission of universal prayer, Our Lord imparted knowledge to His humble bride that she acted upon in a way that was as simple as it was sublime: she immolated herself in union with her Master; she prayed in union with her Master, concentrating all of her intercessory prayer in the assiduous offering of the Savior's merits.

This was already discussed in the chapters pertaining to the Holy Wounds. It remains to examine it more closely in this work of immolation and prayer to which nothing remained foreign.

### The Pope and the Church – Bishops – Priests

Through her daily offering,[1] all of Sister Mary Martha's life was dedicated to God's great cause—the cause of the Church, its pastors and faithful.

Our Lord often renewed to His Servant the promise of the Holy Church's triumph through the power of His Wounds and of the Immaculate Virgin: "My daughter, you must tend well to your duty, which is to offer My Divine Wounds to My Eternal Father, for from this must come the triumph of My Church, which will pass through the hands of My Immaculate Mother."

But, from the beginning, the Divine Master warned against any delusions or equivocations. It would not be the material, visible, and universal triumph certain souls dream about!... Beneath the barque of Peter, the waves shall never submit with a perfect docility; sometimes even, one might tremble before the fury of their agitation... Struggling, always struggling, that is a law of life for the Church: "They do not understand what they are asking when they ask for its triumph... My Church will never have a visible triumph."[2]

However, through struggles and tribulations, the work of Our Lord Jesus Christ, which is the salvation of the world, continues to be accomplished in the Church and by the Church. The work of Our Lord Jesus Christ is accomplished all the more that prayer—which has its place in the divine plan—beseeches more of Heaven's help.

And one can imagine how Heaven allows itself to be especially moved when one prays in the name of the redeeming Wounds. Jesus frequently insisted on this point: "You must draw unceasingly from these Founts for the triumph of My Church."

---

[1] See p. 63.
[2] Meaning a visible, definitive triumph prior to the end of the world.

In an especially troubled time, Sister Mary Martha earnestly pleaded with Our Lord to cover the Sovereign Pontiff with the protection of His Holy Wounds. The Savior was pleased with this prayer. He showed our Sister the grace overflowing onto the Most Holy Father Pius IX, and that the prayers made by the Community greatly contributed to this: "From My Wounds, a special grace goes out to him."

Another day when she was praying for the Church and the conversion of its enemies, Jesus said to her: "How much this prayer is pleasing to Me!... All those who are truly Mine ask for the conversion of the Church's enemies."

The Most Blessed Virgin used the same language in recommending to her child to pray for the great interests of the papacy and for the august Roman Pontiff.

On October 6, 1867 (feast of Our Lady of the Rosary), this good Mother said to her: "I am going to teach you an invocation, and it will please me very much when you say it for the needs of the Holy Church: Our Lady of the Rosary, protect the Holy Father... Our Lady of the Rosary, convert the enemies of the Church and of the Holy Father."

Each day of this month, the fortunate Sister received a visit from the Queen of Heaven who showed her how many graces flowed out onto the world through the Holy Wounds of Jesus and her maternal intercession.

From 1867 until the death of Pius IX,[3] but particularly during the Vatican Council,[4] it is astonishing to see to what extent Sister Mary Martha's life was associated with that of the Church. Our

---

[3] Pope Pius IX died on February 7, 1878.—Trans.
[4] The First Vatican Council opened on December 8, 1869 and was adjourned indefinitely on October 20, 1870.—Trans.

humble Lay Sister followed from a distance, so to speak, the great events whose repercussions Rome was suffering at the time. She shared in the Holy Father's anguish. At the request of Our Lord, she multiplied penances and prayers. She learned from her Master that "His Holiness would remain in the Holy See, but amidst tribulation."

On April 26, 1869, during the invocations to the Holy Wounds that the Community recited each day for the needs of the Church, the Crucified Jesus revealed Himself to His bride. The Divine Blood streamed in great abundance from His Sacred Wounds: "This is for My Vicar Pius IX," He said. And as the Savior's Blood continued to flow, He added: "This is for My Ministers!... for all, even for those who do not ask for light.

"Satan is going to wage the fiercest attacks to try to annihilate the Church.

"A number of lights shall lose light, and a number of those who appear to be pillars shall fall."

At the beginning of December 1869, Our Lord again repeated: "My daughter, you must pray for the Council!... You must redouble your fervor, for it is through the Council that the light must be given."

During this period of time, the hair shirt that our dear Sister wore day and night sometimes became so painful that it was extremely difficult for her to bear. Jesus permitted this increase in sufferings because the needs of the moment required more heroic sacrifices.

In March 1870, the Divine Master announced: "The Council Fathers do not know when it will finish... No one can foresee it..."

From the Sovereign Pontiff, Sister Mary Martha did not separate the Bishops, the Pope's collaborators and his Brothers in Jesus Christ. And, among the bishops, the archdiocesan bishop became the very special object of her filial solicitude. She felt obliged to do more for him than any other. Our Lord made it a duty for her.

It would be interesting to follow her more closely in this respect. Allow us to simply mention a true religious command given by the Sovereign Pastor regarding one of our venerated bishops. He said, "I want this soul to shine like a star in Heaven. I shall only take him from this world when, through your prayers and sufferings, especially through your invocations to the Holy Wounds, you shall have obtained for him this magnificent beauty!"

A few days afterwards, Mary added: "Being an Archbishop, the perfection of this soul must be perfect. Being *your* Archbishop, the Community must adorn him. You must offer prayers, communions, and sufferings. You must cover him with the palms that he must take to Heaven."

In union with the episcopacy, all of the secular and regular clergy benefited from this apostolate that Jesus, the Eternal Priest, asked of His bride. To sustain her ardor in her immolations, Our Lord vividly illuminated her concerning the sublimity of the priest's functions, the greatness of his ministry, the dangers and difficulties awaiting him, his need for greater perfection, and, consequently, his need for more powerful help: "Priests and religious have received from God a great honor through their vocation. They must use it to glorify God by sanctifying themselves and helping to sanctify others.

"He who teaches others, if he does not practice what he teaches, is much guiltier and suffers much more in Purgatory."

On the other hand, the reward is equally incomparable. On the evening of All Souls' Day (November 2, 1869), Sister Mary Martha saw a marvelous procession of souls ascending into Heaven... She could contemplate them, but not approach them. Two of them broke away from this long procession and came to her. They were the souls of two priests! Their beauty defied all human imagination... They said to her: "We have found true happiness, true glory, and true riches!"

The Heavenly Director made his student to understand the greatness of this divine power granted to the successors of the Apostles to forgive sins in His Name and by virtue of His Precious Blood. Our Sister saw it fall on her at the moment of absolution: "I am watering My garden," the Savior once said.

In a vision that filled her with joy, the Virgin Mary appeared to her as the powerful patroness and special guardian of consecrated souls.

Sister Mary Martha was transported to a place that was filled with light and dazzlingly white. "My daughter," the Immaculate said, "this place is my domain, my dwelling place." Beneath Mary's feet stirred a frightful monster with a gaping mouth, from which came forth a thousand sharp cutting instruments. A voice said: "This is for the priests and religious." The good lay sister did not at first understand the meaning of what she saw. The next day, Jesus explained to her that these horrible instruments "represented the diverse temptations by which the devil seeks to wound, deceive, and bring down consecrated souls." Let these souls have recourse to Mary. Her virginal foot ever crushes the head of the serpent.

All of this made a deep impression on our Sister. It goes without saying that in this cult of veneration and in all of her intentions, the confessors and chaplains of the Community were at the forefront. This was notably the case for Canon Bouvier

(1852-1885) and Canon Collonge (1885-1918). Their ministry, their health, and their eternal salvation—all of this was of concern to her. And when we read the manuscripts, it does appear she conveyed to them more than one divine message!

### *Souls – Sinners – The Dying*

Our Lord had taught Sister Mary Martha that "the true triumph of the Church is in souls." In response to this divine lesson, He wanted the cloistered humble one to have a heart as vast as the world and, in this heart, the zeal of an apostle: "Come," He said to her, "come to the conquest of souls!... Come gather souls with Me!... We shall go together everywhere!" A number of times it seemed to her that, being admitted inside the burning Heart of Jesus, He took her to all regions of the globe to gather souls with Him.

It was in this work that the dear missionary spent a portion of her nights, happy when, at her expense, the "harvest" was rich. Giving an account to her Superior one day, she said: "I spent my night gathering souls with the power God gave me through the Holy Wounds of my good Master." It seemed to her at the time that she was harvesting souls as if she were abundantly gathering fruit.

There was an admirable apostolate of perpetual intercession that Jesus asked principally in favor of sinners and of the souls in Purgatory.

"The great misery of this age," He confided to His chosen one, "is that there are too few souls who are saved!... You must pray unceasingly for sinners.

"It is principally for the souls of religious to convert sinners through their prayers, their immolations, and the practice of their Rule."

The Visitation in Chambéry answered the desires of the Divine Master by adopting the Rosary of Mercy devotion. Our Lord did not stop His appeals, however. He more and more insistently presented His Wounds as a source of grace for sinners.

"I have desired for a very long time to see you distribute the fruits of My Redemption.

"For every word you pronounce in the Chaplet of Mercy,[5] I drop a drop of My Blood onto the soul of a sinner.

"Each time you efface the sins of men with My Holy Wounds, you do more than Veronica. What she removed from My Face was light, but sins are very heavy!"

And addressing His chosen bride in particular: "Do you want Me to spread My Blood over sinners, those who abuse it and who trample upon it? Do you want to offer it to My Father for them?"

Then, showing her the multitude of sinners throughout the world: "I show them to you so that you do not waste any time."

These souls one day appeared to her as bogged down in mud. The Immaculate Virgin looked at them with a motherly expression and, taking pity, said to her humble child: "These are good, they are dear. Take them to My Son, to the foot of His throne." And there, Sister Mary Martha saw them, soaked in the Blood of Our Lord, suddenly arrayed in great beauty.

One of the things that saddens Jesus most and provokes most His anger is the violation of Sunday rest.

---

[5] See chap. 10, n. 5.

One Saturday, Sister Mary Martha was visiting our modest cemetery, reciting over each grave one *Eternal Rest* and her dear invocations to the Holy Wounds, when she suddenly heard complaints from the Divine Master: "My daughter, there are Christians who are preparing themselves for work tomorrow… Tell your Superior to make reparation to Me." The next day, Sunday, as she was going again to the garden, the Savior said to her: "Lift your eyes and see." She looked and saw, in the fields surrounding the monastery, a great number of people busy working: "Behold, My daughter, what draws down the chastisements of God."

Threats were sometimes joined to the complaints: "On Judgment Day, when men see everything I did for them during My life on earth; when they see My works, My sufferings, and My love, they will be very sorry for not having better profited from them!" Or instead it was a striking vision of the Justice of God provoked by the sins of the world. In an indescribable suffering, feeling as though the weight of Divine Justice and of the sins of her brethren was pressing down upon her, she distressingly cried out, humbling herself: "My God, do not look at our misery, but look at Your Mercy!" And she began anew the invocations to the Holy Wounds, which appeased the Justice of God: "Offer them to Me often to gain Me sinners, for I am hungry for souls."

When paschal retreats and missions were given at the parish church of Lémenc or in the other parishes of the archdiocese, our Sister had to redouble her prayers and sacrifices—it was necessary to aid the work of the missionaries, to prepare the ways for divine grace, and to make up for deficiencies! "My Mother and I, we shall tread the winepress," Jesus said, "there will be some who have worked much and who will have nothing… There are souls who receive life, and others who remain on the ground; it is for you to take them and give them life.

"My daughter, you must lead the souls to My feet, you must bring them close to Me. I shall be in their midst—like a good Shepherd—to convert them."

To renew the zeal of His chosen one, Our Lord sometimes allowed her to see the marvels at work in souls.

On March 27, 1868, the Community was praying in particular for the paschal retreat at Lémenc: "My daughter," the Divine Master said, "I want to have you come out of the enclosure." These words initially frightened the innocent child greatly! She then felt herself transported in spirit inside the parish church. Our Lord showed Himself to her, taking in His hand a chalice full of His Precious Blood: "My daughter, I want you to be a witness to the favors I am going to grant." And Sister Mary Martha saw the Savior placing within the souls a drop of His Divine Blood. She even had the unspeakable consolation of seeing Him do this for the souls of her father and mother as these words came forth from the divine lips: "The graces I give in this manner are not wasted."

In favor of the dying, our Sister's zeal seemed to outdo itself even further.

"When one adorns My altars," the good Master said, "one pleases Me greatly. But when one wins Me souls for Paradise, My consolation is incomparably greater.

"You must often offer the merits of My Holy Wounds for those who are dying during the night or during the course of the day."

In the manuscripts, we find details of certain nights spent accompanying souls whom Jesus showed her as close to entering their eternity: "You are in charge of all of these souls; you must obtain them a happy death."

Souls! Sister Mary Martha took "charge" of them with all the more fervor since their salvation and perfection glorified God. She had so well understood that she was on earth only "to procure the glory of God and to make Him loved." And in this, as in everything, Our Lord enlightened her and spurred her on: "My daughter, I desire constantly that men profit from the fruit of My Redemption. But, faithful or not, My glory must issue from it!"

Three brilliant rays coming from the Holy Wounds of Jesus appeared one day, in the eyes of our Sister, to envelop the souls saved by the merits of the Redeemer. Whoever had contributed to procuring them this blessing also received a great glory from the greater glory it gave to God: "By helping souls to benefit from the fruits of My Passion," the Savior explained, "you extend the Kingdom of God!" Passionately, the fervent heart of the humble cloistered missionary responded with this cry that fully expressed her: "My Jesus, I thirst for souls for Your glory!"

### The Souls in Purgatory

Sister Mary Martha's apostolic flame was not extinguished at the gates of the tomb. A great advocate for sinners and the dying, our Sister was no less so for the souls in Purgatory. Moreover, these souls continuously begged for her sufferings and prayers: "See!... Bring us relief!... Offer the Holy Wounds of Jesus for us."

In turn, she repeated to Our Lord: "See!... Bring them relief through Your Divine Wounds."

To bring them relief, such indeed is Jesus's desire. He waits for prayers to Him. He urged Sister Mary Martha to do this. He addressed His bride with these amazing words of kindness: "A poor creature like you, when united to Me, can do everything! It shakes Purgatory and it fills Heaven!"

He assigned her a place for her mission of supplication: "You are not of this world: your life must be suspended between Heaven and Purgatory… You must see yourself as being at the gate of Purgatory to help souls leave it… and at the gate of Heaven to take souls and help them enter therein."

He continued His appeals with His encouragements: "I give My riches to the humble and to the little so that they might be paid back to Me through the deliverance of the souls in Purgatory.

"One sees sinners and one thinks more about praying for them. As for the souls in Purgatory, not being seen, the world often forgets them. Few are the souls who would not go to Purgatory. I want you to pray much."

And the prayer that Jesus recommended was the one that directly appeals to the merits of His Passion: "My daughter, look to My Wounds. Offer them for the souls in Purgatory. The sufferings of My Holy Passion—behold the great remedy for these poor souls; but you must apply these merits to them."

One night, Sister Mary Martha, immersed in fervent prayer, asked for the relief of her friends in Purgatory. Jesus Crucified, appearing before her eyes, said to her: "I want to grant you a soul for each one of My Wounds." And in spaced-out intervals, our dear Sister saw a soul issue forth from the Wounds of Jesus and fly up into Heaven: the first and second exited from His Sacred Feet, and the last one from His Right Hand: "This one was the costliest."

Need it be said? Among the suffering souls, there are some who are dearer to the heart of a religious—these are the souls of her own Sisters. Sister Mary Martha prayed and suffered for them more particularly, and the Blessed Virgin expressed her satisfaction to her: "The souls of your Sisters in Purgatory are my daughters. I take great pleasure in hearing you pray for their deliverance… It pains me to see them in this fire!... I am Queen and I want these souls to reign with me! Despite all our power, my Son and I cannot deliver them—they must expiate… But you can so easily relieve them and open up Heaven to them by offering the Holy Wounds to God the Father on their behalf."

To her prayers, Sister Mary Martha joined the immolation of her days and nights in the manner we have already described.

One evening, the Victim of Jesus, stretched out on the ground and laden with all her instruments of penance, was suffering in an unusual manner. A number of souls from Purgatory appeared to her: "Your entire day tomorrow will be for us."

That day was a horrible day—one of those days during which the Lord, like with the holy man Job, allowed Satan to afflict His servant, a day being completely abandoned by Jesus!

In the evening, the Bridegroom returned more affectionate than ever and opened to her His Sacred Heart: "Behold your salvation," He said. "Through the severe temptation you suffered and through your abandonment, a great number of souls in Purgatory were freed. Your sufferings were necessary for this."

One year on the day prior to the Ascension, Jesus similarly said to her: "My daughter, do not expect to enjoy this day, for many souls must, through your sufferings, get to Heaven to be present for My triumph." She in fact suffered greatly. But what happiness the following night, and what a reward! "I had you suffer for some souls whom I wanted to get out of Purgatory. And now that they are in Heaven, you are going to enjoy the vision of My Blessed."

Another precious means our Sister used in this ministry of charity was the offering of her actions in union with the Holy Wounds. One evening when it was time to go to supper, she felt herself surrounded by suffering souls who said to her: "We are going with you to the refectory so that you might give us to eat." At the same time, an interior light made her to understand the meaning of such a request: for their deliverance, these souls were soliciting actions made in union with the Wounds of the Savior. Another day, experiencing an irresistible urge to withdraw into her heart, she perceived something like a chain linking the earth to Purgatory and Purgatory to Heaven. And the Savior Himself said to her: "I want all of your hearts to be one with Heaven and Purgatory."

A yet more efficacious means: Holy Mass and Holy Communion. We shall simply point out in this regard that, in accordance with the desire expressed by Our Lord, the Community offered Holy Communion every Monday for the souls in Purgatory and for the good of the Church.

We shall also mention that a great number of our Sisters had taken up the habit of offering the Holy Wounds between the two elevations at Holy Mass, something for which the souls in Purgatory expressed their grateful joy: "Now every day is Monday! It is a feast day for us every day!"

Finally, let us speak of indulgences.

Like Christ Himself, the Church loves the souls in Purgatory, and through the power it has from Christ, it offers us, in indulgences, a means to deliver them.

Sister Mary Martha was too much of a loving daughter and too supernaturally enlightened to not have recourse to this means.

If the Holy Wounds invocations were perpetually on her lips, who can tell the number of indulgenced prayers, *Out of the Depths* and *Eternal Rests*, that she unceasingly joined with them?

And when All Souls' Day arrived or, better yet, the great Portiuncula Indulgence, who can express how eagerly the former tertiary took advantage of the Church's spiritual largesse! This feast on the second of August, which recalls the anniversary of her religious profession, was therefore a day of fervor for all, in the service of her suffering friends. She dedicated to them all the time she could spare, and it is said that her number of visits to the church sometimes reached a hundred.

Besides the satisfaction of responding to the desires of the Heart of Jesus, our dear Sister received other encouragements in accomplishing "her task." It seems Our Lord granted her a kind of knowledge of the sufferings endured in Purgatory and enabled her to contemplate the joy of the Elect upon delivered souls' arrival in Heaven. He also made her to understand that there is no such thing as ingratitude in Heaven: "My little Mary Martha," one of the souls in Heaven said, "look at all of these souls whom you have delivered through your prayers and sufferings!... They cannot all come and thank you now, but they will come to meet you when you depart from this world."

# CHAPTER 26

## TRIALS

*Contradictions – Fears of Delusion – Abandonment –Attacks from the Devil*

BVIOUSLY, the life of Sister Mary Martha could not have progressed without complications. That is easy to understand, as there was a combination of things beyond the realm of the ordinary that could only astound.

Her long five-year fast, which was diversely interpreted; different measures taken by authority, and which sometimes ran counter to human judgment; this "practice" of two new invocations; the silence maintained by the Superiors and Sister Mary Martha herself concerning her graces; a hard-to-define, enigmatic "something" that enveloped our Sister like a veil; and a sense of the supernatural joined to a certain astonishment at persistent imperfections—all of these things hardly allowed one to form a nice clean opinion. All of these things, coming together as though unconsciously in people's minds, led, in 1875, to a rather painful incident.

The canonical visit was approaching. It would be the first one made by our new Archbishop. Sister Mary Martha warned her confidantes: "It will be horrible; but afterwards, you will be consoled."

Some Sisters, in fact, who were undoubtedly well-intentioned but perhaps imprudent, reported to His Excellency several things

that seemed to them inexplicable in Sister Mary Martha—
inexplicable and unacceptable. God permitted the Prelate,
without first thinking to clarify the facts with the Superior, to
believe it necessary to give satisfaction to the malcontents and
to state publicly, in front of the entire House assembled together,
the way he saw things, and in a rather severe manner!

The trial was painful. Our Mothers, however, humbly obeyed
the orders received and drank the bitter chalice in silence.

One can imagine what the prayers of our Sister were at the
time, whom the Archbishop had forbidden from continuing the
practice of daily communion... It did not take long for the
situation to be resolved. Canon Bouvier, our chaplain, knew so
well how to plead the cause of this humble and mortified soul
before His Excellency, and the pious Prelate gave him complete
freedom to do as he saw fit...

This incident thus came to an end.

But Sister Mary Martha faced other trials throughout the
course of her life. And it is of these that we now wish to speak.

Just as a gold refiner purifies this precious metal in the
furnace, so does God try this incomparable gold in the Church
that is the souls of the saints.

One of their frequent trials—and not the least painful—is the
fear of being the plaything of mankind's eternal enemy.

On one hand, they are well aware that the devil sometimes
transforms himself into an angel of light to cunningly lead souls
into error and pride. On the other hand, humility shields them
from believing themselves the object of the Most High's
predilections.

This was for Sister Mary Martha a sometimes very difficult suffering, but one from which Our Lord never wanted to free her completely.

On the days following the most distinguished of favors, the soul of our dear Sister almost always suffered some interior torments. It was also true that Jesus almost always brought her a sweet and comforting word.

After a night during which the anguish and the struggle had completely exhausted her, Jesus said: "It is I Who am Strength, I shall communicate it to you... I am satisfied with your sufferings." Sister Mary Martha immediately found herself strengthened and invigorated for work.

Since then, our Very Honorable Mother asserted, the suffering still continued; but it was not as profound as the first year; it remained on the peripheries of her soul; deep inside, it was no longer possible for our Sister to doubt that God was leading her.

One incident, however, would again plunge the dear Privileged One into extreme distress. During one of the Ember day periods in 1870, after having spoken some words about her interior state to an extraordinary confessor, the latter briefly responded that her path might well be nothing but an illusion and a deception. One can imagine the effect these words had on Sister Mary Martha. Our Blessed Father [St. Francis de Sales] took pity on the poor afflicted one and came to reassure her: "My daughter, if I could return to earth to make laws, I would preserve those that I made; and for you, I would give one in particular. I shall help you to follow your path and I shall give you special advice even though I am no longer on earth."

The ruses employed by the devil to trouble Sister Mary Martha were as countless as they were crafty. Sometimes he insinuated that she was outside of the Rule and a bad example to the Sisters… that she was going to suffer in the other world if she did not change course… Sometimes he portrayed her supposed "graces" to her as mere figments of her imagination: "Hypocrite! Witch! You deceive and you are deceived… Your Superiors see it clearly, but they do not want to tell you," and a thousand other similar things that greatly frightened the poor victim.

Sometimes the devil accused her of taking excessive care of her body: "You love life too much, you will lose it… You love taking care of yourself too much, you will go to burn in hell."[1]

Or he would even make her believe that she had succumbed to pride: "You think yourself a Saint, but there is no Heaven for you."

"Well, then I shall place myself at the feet of Jesus and of the Saints!" the humble Sister replied. Then she was troubled and feared having in fact showed some pride through this response.

"Yes, you have committed the sin of the Angels," the liar very quickly affirmed, "you will go to hell with them."

The devil's tactics aimed at the same time to distance her from those who could enlighten her: "You are a cross for your Superiors, do not tell them anything!" Once, he even whispered into her head a thousand critical thoughts against authority. The suggestions were so strong that it seemed to our poor Sister that she was consenting to these temptations, which threw her into extreme anguish. Also feeling herself held back by an invisible power that prevented her from having recourse to our Mother, she went in tears to take refuge before the Blessed Sacrament.

---

[1] "There is no one who thinks less about her body than this poor child," our Very Honorable Mother Thérèse-Eugénie wrote in parentheses.

Jesus welcomed her with this gentle reproach: "My child, are you forgetting Me?... If you had recourse to Me with confidence, I would serve you as Mother... if you turned to Me, I would deliver you... You must keep close to Me and pray, and then Satan will go away..."

How touching is Jesus's kindness towards souls! He allows them to suffer, for suffering is useful and necessary for them. But one would say that He Himself endures the pains He permits, so eagerly does He come to alleviate them as soon as He can do so without taking away the merit. It is the spectacle that the Bridegroom of Love offers us in these dealings with His favorite bride. Let us consider it in the following telling incident:

One evening when the anguish was more intense, Sister Mary Martha turned to Our Lord and said: "O my good Master, would it be possible for a heart to perish that loves You so much, speaks with You so often, and unites herself to You daily in Communion?"

Hardly had she uttered this loving complaint when the temptation vanished. The sweet voice of Jesus made itself heard: "No, My beloved one," He said as He drew her to His Heart, "you shall be here for time and for eternity. All those who have loved Me and have lived your life are now with Me in Paradise."

The Divine Master did not omit subjecting His bride to another great test of love: absence. The absence of Jesus threw Sister Mary Martha into a veritable agony. One could thus imagine her roaming everywhere, seeming to ask like the lover in the Canticle of Canticles: "Have you seen my Beloved?"

This absence was sometimes punishment for a slight infidelity. Jesus, upon returning, brought pardon and joy with these words: "I have purified everything in you through this abandonment."

At other times, love alone was the cause: "love makes lovers alike." "My daughter, I wept in the Garden of Olives and on the Cross, in My great abandonment," He told her, after she had gone several days without an answer to her sighs and tears. The same lesson was repeated to her by His Immaculate Mother: "I come to announce to you Jesus's abandonment, so that you might participate in His divine abandonment on the Cross when He was abandoned by His Father."

In August 1869, after having allowed her to contemplate in Heaven, amidst the Blessed, the Father and the Son in Their glory and power, Our Lord suddenly made Himself no longer seen or felt for an entire week, leaving Sister Mary Martha subject to inexpressible suffering. When Jesus returned, He informed her of the reasons for this abandonment: "On the Cross, at the height of My sufferings, I was all alone… That is why I wanted you to suffer thus."

He further said to her: "Love hides to make itself sought… I am returning, but do not expect it to be forever. I shall go away again, and it will be useful for you, for you would not love Me so much if I always remained visibly present to you."

A second intention of Jesus's was to lead His servant to perfect interior detachment. For this reason, the good Master left her in absolute abandonment for fifteen consecutive days. Little accustomed to this behavior, Sister Mary Martha looked pitiful… The words she had spoken to her Superior shortly beforehand, "When God wants a soul to suffer, nothing can comfort her," were to be perfectly fulfilled in her.

Lastly, Jesus also imposed this martyrdom of absence on His bride for the salvation of souls: "My daughter, through the severe temptation you suffered and through your interior abandonment, a number of souls have been converted and a number of souls in Purgatory have been delivered... Your sufferings were necessary for this."

We shall not describe any more of these moving scenes, these agonies, and these raptures... and the ineffable returns following the sorrowful abandonments. Every soul that loves with a true love must understand them and experience them. We would be speaking in vain to anyone else.

\*\*\*

Another trial, common to all the children of Adam, proceeds from the temptations and desires of our fallen nature.

For Sister Mary Martha, the importunity of these temptations was increased tenfold by the malice of Lucifer, who hoped to use them, if not to make her fall into evil, to at least disturb her in her task and to halt her progress.

Thus, as we have already said, he made a mockery of her practices of piety, notably the offering of the Holy Wounds. Sometimes he sought to prevent her from fulfilling her duty: "Do not go back to your work, it will damn you." He worried her about her health to prevent her from doing services: "Do not go to the garden anymore, it will upset your health." There were also thoughts of discouragement and incitements to discontent: "Ask for rest. Your Mother is hard on you." And even suggestions against the faith: "Of what good are your communions?" On one day, he even came to her five times in bodily form, keeping himself at a distance and repeating: "There is no God!... Of what good are your prayers when there is no God..."

Sister Mary Martha forcefully protested: "I believe that there is a God and that He is my Husband!... He is my Husband!... He is my food…" At this response, the devil disappeared into thin air.

The evil one also tried to inspire her to pride through harmful insinuations: "The Community is quite fortunate to have you."

"Yes," Jesus answered, preserving His bride by adding a corrective, "quite fortunate on account of your ignorance."

Only once did Our Lord permit attacks against the purity of this innocent soul: "There is nothing in you but lies. You have committed many sins against the sixth commandment." Such an accusation troubled the innocent child. She ran to ask her Superior: "What are these sins?… I do not know what they are."

The devil's attacks were not limited to these repeated temptations. He made use of all kinds of vexations to torture her in soul and body. The Superiors, who were eyewitnesses to these things, painfully wrote down the persecutions and wicked treatment that the infernal enemy, with God's permission, inflicted upon her. This ferocity especially manifested itself in the great needs of the Church or of individual souls.

In the midst of these combats, Sister Mary Martha resisted with all the courage of her faith and love. If there were particularly painful times, Jesus intervened to support her weakness, encouraging her with His words or giving her the consolation of His divine presence: "Come, My child, hide yourself in My Heart. It was there that My Mother drew her humility… Follow the examples of humility I give you in My Holy Infancy and you shall overcome the devil."

Even when the diabolical attacks were at their strongest, Our Lord maintained an all-powerful sense of duty within her soul: "My daughter, always go where duty calls you."

"As soon as the time comes for her to serve the students," the Superiors noted, "our Sister regains enough strength and presence of mind to do so."

Our Lord reminded her that it was for souls that she was suffering: "My beloved, if I have you suffer without respite, it is because the wicked themselves do not sleep either."

Sometimes He even made known to her the prize for these crucifying sufferings. One time among others, Sister Mary Martha learned in advance of the sickness and subsequent death of a gentleman of the parish whom she named to her Superior and for whose salvation Our Lord permitted her to undergo a veritable martyrdom. This soul came to thank her: "It was for me that you suffered so much. The devil was enraged at losing me. I owe you my salvation—my place was in hell and I am in Heaven, through the merits of the Wounds of Jesus that you invoked for me." The details of this death were able to be verified by our Very Honorable Mother and were found to be completely accurate (May-June 1869).

On the fourth of September of the same year, the manuscript reports, the spirit of darkness waged a fierce and terrible conflict against our child. At one o'clock in the morning, being both physically and interiorly broken, she was weighed down on the floor exhausted, there to spend the rest of the night… Suddenly, the simple cell was filled with light… God the Father appeared, as well as Our Lord on the Cross. Jesus said: "Father, look at Me… I am in this state, laden with all the sins of the world." Then, looking down with love at the innocent victim stretched out beneath His feet, the sweet Redeemer added: "You, also, are laden with the sins of men." Sister Mary Martha then stretched out her arms to offer her sorrowful Calvary in union with that of the Divine Crucified, while from her heart, as an echo, this cry sprang forth: "My God, I also pray for all of your creatures…"

But the time of suffering was over; a profound consolation penetrated her heart. An extreme hunger for God took hold of her: "My God, come quickly… Give me this Bread with which one hungers no more… give me this water with which one thirsts no more!... I offer you my heart and the hearts of my Mothers… My God, repay them for what they do for me… Set their hearts on fire with Your holy Love!... Oh, come, come, divine Jesus!" All of a sudden, she cried out: "Oh, He is here, the Divine Child!" Yes, He was there, responding to the impassioned plea of His bride, giving Himself to her. And feeling the effects of this wondrous Communion, the blessed seer, savoring her treasure, said from time to time: "He is setting me on fire with love like a burning ray." The ecstasy lasted until daybreak.

# CHAPTER 27

# SPECIAL GRACES

## *Extraordinary Visions*

WAS it in her love for Our Lord that Sister Mary Martha received additional lights? We find in her knowledge that would be difficult to explain naturally. It seems God gave her the gift of reading into the future.

Various examples have already been encountered throughout these pages, incidentally reported when focusing on other matters. We shall elaborate further.

At the time of Pope Pius IX's great difficulties, particularly between 1866 and 1870, Sister Mary Martha, uninformed by natural means of current events, was living them in her heart before the Tabernacle. The same day as the Battle of Mentana, she learned of the papal troops' victory (to which, Jesus said, the invocations to the Holy Wounds had contributed); she made this known to her Superior, who subsequently received confirmation of the news in the parlor. As for the Vatican Council, we have already noted how she was following it from a distance, so to speak.[1]

As early as January 15, 1878, the death of Pius IX was announced to her through a mysterious vision, the meaning of which she did not understand at the time.

---

[1] See chap. 25.

245

"A great procession of Holy Pontiffs who had come from Heaven were returning there, taking to the heavenly abode a Saint wearing a golden robe of extraordinary brightness. The latter, however, remained at the gate to Paradise while the other Pontiffs told our Sister, 'We are leaving him still, but soon he will be with us.' After this, they disappeared in glory.

"Each day, she had the same vision, and as all her fear was that God was calling to Himself our worthy Chaplain, Father Bouvier, who was unwell at the time, she thought it was the announcement of his death.

"On January 29, she understood that the glorious troop of Pontiffs would soon return to get their holy Friend.

"Finally, on February 9, during the Stations of the Cross being prayed for our Holy Father Pope Pius IX, the soul of this august Deceased appeared, all glorious, to Sister Mary Martha, who then recognized the one whom God had showed her dressed in gold at the gate to Paradise. He had gone straight to Heaven, through the merits of the Holy Wounds of Jesus" (Manuscript).

In what concerned France, Sister Mary Martha knew in advance about the [Franco-Prussian] War of 1870: "I want to melt the world," Our Lord said to her among other things in the month of May. As the Superior did not understand these words, she refrained from writing them down. A few weeks later, Our Lord came back to this: "These words were not written down, I want them to be." Then, in the month of August, He clearly explained their meaning.

As early as January 21, 1871, she learned of the horrors of the Commune: "There will be massacres of priests and religious... I shall not permit this to happen in your land [of Savoy]."

As for the internal history of the Community, she provided a great number of surprising insights, forecasts, and predictions. Sister Mary Martha's Superior and Directress attested to these things with an astonishment that is easy to understand.

Our Sister sometimes seemed to "read consciences."

"We believed we had identified in a certain soul three points on which she had to work. We pointed out two of them, not yet daring to address the third. On the morning of the following day, our dear Privileged One came humbly to bring up this omission: 'Mother, Our Lord says that in the soul of Sister N., there are three points on which she must work.' I was stunned," concluded the Superior (Manuscript).

Our dear Sister sometimes brought our Mother advice—on behalf of the good Master, she said—concerning the interior dispositions and needs of one of us. And when the Superior used this advice, she invariably received a response like this: "How true it is, Mother, what Your Charity is telling me! One would think the good God lets you read what is happening in my soul."

It was sometimes the soul of the Superior herself who became, for Sister Mary Martha, as transparent as crystal: "Mother, our good Master told me to pray for you because you are in such a disposition today." Or even: "Mother, Your Charity is upset about this or that thing... Our Lord is not pleased."

"And what our beloved Sister told us was always perfectly accurate. Not having communicated to anyone my interior dispositions, I could see that God Himself had revealed them to our child! And this happened multiple times" (Manuscript).

For certain things, the Servant of God could also see into the future. Thus, our Mothers were usually warned by her of the more or less imminent death of our deceased Sisters. At the time, this was a secret among the Superiors. Their manuscripts have since revealed this to us.

One month prior to the death of our Sister Marie-Justine Gojon (died December 9, 1866), Our Lord warned Sister Mary Martha that He planned to call her to Himself. "Ask Me," He told her, "to not enter into judgment with this soul." Then, He showed her, in all its details, an incident in the life of this dear Sister when, as the bursar, she had been too severe with her neighbor. It was twenty-five years ago that this incident had happened, and our Very Honorable Sister Marie-Alexis Blanc was the only one in the House who knew how the matter unfolded. Sister Mary Martha specified the year, named the persons, etc., to the amazement of her Mistress. She suffered much in the days preceding Sister Marie-Justine's death. To console His little bride, the Divine Master then showed her this soul ascending into Heaven, fully purified and glorious. Shortly thereafter, the Deceased herself came to thank our Privileged One for her prayers and the sufferings endured for her sake.

Since that time, not only was Sister Mary Martha warned of impending deaths, but her interior gaze followed the dearly departed to the hereafter. Thus it was for one of the dearest members of both her spiritual and natural family: her sister Mariette, who in religious life had become Sister Marie-Claudine.

Initially inclined towards frivolity, albeit while preserving a simple and pure soul, this dear younger sister owed her religious vocation to the prayers of her elder sister.[2] Intelligent and

---

[2] As a witness moved by the happiness of the dear novice at the time of her profession, Mariette had asked for her elder sister to obtain for her, beneath the burial cloth, the grace to one day share it. She was fully answered, becoming remarkably pious from that point forward, and not ceasing to aspire to the total gift of herself to Our Lord.

endowed with good judgment, with all the qualities fitting for her station, and with a special skillfulness, she made herself very useful in the diverse jobs where obedience placed her. But the Community above all based its hope on the virtues it saw her acquire each day.

One night in September 1870, the Servant of God was, as usual, before the Most Blessed Sacrament. Our Lord revealed to her that He was soon going to call to Himself our dear little Sister Marie-Claudine, who was not yet two years professed and twenty-five years of age. She could see her clothed in white, lying lifeless on the altar like a victim... but with a radiant beauty. The Blessed surrounded and contemplated her, and Jesus said: "Now she will die no more!"

Sister Mary Martha understood that it was incumbent upon her to complete her sister's crown and to adorn her for the Eternal Wedding. She prayed and suffered much.

In the course of October, an imprudence, caused by a dedication that did not know its own limits, brought on the illness from which Sister Marie-Claudine would never recover. On May 17, 1871, she received the Last Sacraments. On the twentieth, in the afternoon, a voice from Heaven warned Sister Mary Martha that the hour of separation was about to toll: "Through the great sufferings you have endured in body and soul, you have finished her crown and paid her debt." At these words, she felt a great interior peace.

Towards four o'clock, she placed a flower at the feet of the Blessed Virgin in her little oratory: "My good Mother, I offer you this flower for my sister Marie-Claudine."

---

It is a kind of tradition in the Visitation that the prayers of the blessed professed, who is covered with a burial cloth—a symbol of separation from both the world and herself—have a special efficacy.

"I am going to get her," Mary answered. Our Sister promptly went up to the infirmary, where she saw the Immaculate Virgin leaning towards the dying one with our deceased Mother Marie-Pauline Deglapigny.

At the end of Matins, surrounded by her Mothers in Heaven and her Mothers on earth, and before the envying eyes of her beloved sister, the dear dying one was taken up into Heaven.

Her immediate entry into Beatitude was shown to Sister Mary Martha, already kneeling at the choir door for her holy vigil: "Thank you, my sister!... If my crown is so beautiful, I largely owe it to you."

The vision of this soul's happiness rekindled in our Privileged One an ardent desire for death and Heaven; and bursting into tears, she begged her sister to obtain for her the grace to go join her: "It is I who ought to have left first since I am the older one."

"Your crown will be even much more beautiful than mine because you are saving souls through the Holy Wounds of Jesus... You must work still, and for you and for me... When your task is finished, I shall come get you."

Sister Mary Martha often saw her again, always adorned in unparalleled beauty: "I am a Bride and I follow the Lamb everywhere," said the blessed soul of this dear younger sister in a ravishing voice.

It was similar for our Sister Marie-Anastase Jay (1880). A voice from Heaven warned Sister Mary Martha: "A Sister shall fall ill with consumption and not recover." Sister Marie-Anastase, seized by this illness, succumbed the following fifteenth of October. One week prior to her death, on the burial day of Archbishop Pichenot[3] (for whom this Sister was the first novice and spiritual daughter), the venerable Deceased, appearing to our Privileged One, said to her: "You are going to suffer eight days for Sister Marie-Anastase. All the prayers offered for her healing have served for her sanctification... your sufferings will be for her Purgatory... It is not much, eight days... and at the same hour as I, she shall go into the grave." Exactly eight days to the hour after His Excellency's funeral, we accompanied our young Sister to her final resting place.

It was also the same for many others. So much so that our successive Mothers had adopted the habit of asking the humble Lay Sister when a Sister was nearing her last: "Will it be today?" Our Sister would give a simple answer. Never was she mistaken. And this despite her work keeping her at a distance from the dying Sisters and not permitting her to follow the progress of the illness.

Whenever God called to Himself one of our children from the boarding school, it was rare for "good Sister Martha" to be unaware of it.

Asked by one of her confidantes, our beaming and beloved Mother Jeanne-Marie-Anne Spinella, who was the very long-serving boarding school headmistress and is now deceased, gave this response: "Every time I expressed to her my concerns about a sick student, Sister Mary Martha told me what the illness's outcome would be, and what she said happened every time."

Our dear Sister's lights extended to members of her family.

In 1880, the death of the youngest of her brothers was announced to her in an astonishing manner. There was being

---

[3] His Excellency Pierre-Anastase Pichenot was Archbishop of Chambéry from 1873 until his death on October 5, 1880.—Trans.

prepared, it appeared to her, a magnificent wedding feast, in which a great number of guests were participating. The Master of the house was distributing a bread of perfect whiteness and exquisite taste. "There is no wedding feast on earth like this one," he said to her, and he invited her to prepare each piece herself.

A few days later, Sister Mary Martha learned of the death of her brother, whose blessed soul immediately appeared to her: "It was I who was the guest at the wedding feast that you had to prepare through your prayers and sufferings. Yet my life conformed to holiness: I was good to my neighbor, I was meek and patient; I fulfilled my duties as a Christian and was not attached to the goods of this world... My task was finished, I went straight to Heaven... as for you, you must suffer still and fulfill God's Will to the very end—you are chosen from on high to accomplish unknown designs."

In the following year, it was her father's turn. Our Sister knew he was ill and asked God for this good father's recovery, if such was His Will. "Let him come, it is time," an intimate voice said to her, which seemed to be that of her brothers and sister in Heaven. "Even when they announce to you that he is doing better, do not believe it." On January 2, 1882, after Holy Communion, she heard the voice of her father himself: "You will no longer see me vibrant, ruddy, and healthy!... At this moment, my body is pale and icy."

As she was doubting this was truly the voice of her father, someone rang at the door. "It is for you... they come to announce my death," the voice continued. It indeed was for her: the eldest of her brothers asked for her in order to communicate the sad news. Sister Mary Martha was indescribably grieved over this, her Superior wrote, though soon consoled, for the soul of the dear deceased said to her: "I am very happy. I am laden with merits and riches through the Holy Wounds of Jesus!"

Always the Holy Wounds! It was the pledge of salvation that Our Lord had long offered to His Servant, one day adding: "A religious soul who goes to the other world without having obtained both of her parents' salvation has not performed her task."

After the deaths of the former Mothers who were the depositaries of her secrets, although always silent and more and more steeped in the hidden life, Sister Mary Martha respectfully approached the Superior from time to time, telling her what Our Lord had undoubtedly demanded her to make known. She then withdrew without adding another word, and without worrying whether attention was paid to her words.

At the moment when prudence wanted us to ensure ourselves shelter in the land of exile,[4] we first had recourse to the compassionate charity of our monasteries in Italy. The Visitation in Turin was to receive a certain number of us.

On February 24, 1903, Sister Mary Martha, approaching our Very Honorable Mother Jeanne-Marie-Anne with a pained and concerned expression, said to her: "Mother, something serious is happening in Turin!" Then, on the next day, we received the message announcing the death of our Very Honorable Mother Thérèse-Angélique Crotti de Castiglione and, shortly afterwards, the news that, for various reasons independent of their good will, our dear Sisters could no longer offer the

---

[4] In the earliest years of the twentieth century, beginning with the Associations Bill of 1901, the French government enacted oppressive measures targeting religious orders. Many religious communities were suppressed, expelled from their monasteries, and forced into exile.—Trans.

promised hospitality... We had to look elsewhere for a safe haven.

A few years later, a rather important decision had to be made about proposals coming from the outside. The matter was completely unknown to the Community, as the Superior had only spoken about it with her council. The question had been debated in the morning. How surprised our Very Honorable Mother was when, upon leaving the refectory, she saw Sister Mary Martha approach her and very humbly say, "Mother, Our Lord says you must not do that," and then, even more humbly, withdraw very quickly back to her place!

Jesus thus continued to lovingly watch over us and to inform His faithful Bride of His desires for us... and we were unaware of it!

How many times, since her death, have we heard her last Superiors express regret at not having questioned the dear Privileged One more often! But it was part of God's plan to keep her hidden, according to the promise He had made to her.[5]

### Ecstasies

We know the spiritual consolations and intimate joys of Sister Mary Martha. We have read the delightful and moving pages that are filled with visits from the Infant Jesus, appeals from Jesus Crucified, conversations with God the Father, and encouragements from the Most Blessed Virgin and the Saints.

These favors usually left the blessed Lay Sister in control of herself, free to tend to the duties of her work which she

---

[5] Our Mother Jeanne-Marie-Anne Spinella admitted that, several times, when about to question our Honorable Sister and former Mother Marie-Alexis regarding Sister Mary Martha, she felt herself held back by a certain inexplicable reserve.

continued to fulfill, her eyes interiorly fixed on the heavenly vision.

But there were also times when she was as though entirely absorbed in God and deprived of the use of her external senses. It was the irresistible attraction of God and even perhaps ecstasy. Most often the cause was a vision of Our Lord in a state of extraordinary glory.

Did our Sister really see the Divine Master with her bodily eyes? "We had been forbidden to question her," said one of her companions regarding this subject, "but one day I did not adhere to this and I said to her, 'Sister Mary Martha, Your Charity sees Our Lord, no?' She answered me, 'No, I do not see Him, but it is as if I were seeing Him.'"

However, it did sometimes seem to her that she was having a vision of the Sacred Humanity of Jesus with her bodily eyes. In her accounts, we find expressions such as these to make the distinction: "I saw with the eyes of my soul," or even very rarely: "This time, I saw Him with my bodily eyes."

Regardless, our Mothers noted a number of very striking cases where there was a "suspension of the senses." For those of us who were witnesses to this, the publication of the handwritten notes brought back specific memories and also gave a new meaning to the happenings.

"On April 22, 1871, beginning at dawn, our dear child found herself powerfully drawn to her God. She saw Our Lord and, when the time came for Communion, heard Him calling her: "Come quickly, My Bride!" These words inflamed her with love... The morning was passed in the most intimate and sensible union. During the day's Chapter, after having confessed her faults, she lost use of her senses and collapsed. After two hours, she came to like someone awaking from a deep sleep.

"Questioned by us, she responded in a few words that she had seen Our Lord with His glorious Wounds... 'Oh, when shall we see them in Heaven!' And addressing our Very Honorable Mother: 'I can't stand up any longer... I don't have the strength to endure the sight of my good Master. He leans towards me and looks at me with such great love!'"

The Savior did, however, give her enough strength to endure His divine presence, which she continued to enjoy while going back to her ordinary work.

"On the twentieth of June of the same year, the Community, gathered at the foot of the oratory dedicated to the Sacred Heart, was making the preparatory novena for the feast day. Our Lord again appeared to His humble Servant with His Wounds, radiating such glory that she immediately lost all consciousness and fell to the ground. She had to be carried to her bed. She had a ruddy and heavenly face and appeared to be enjoying a beneficial repose. Several of our Sisters, believing her ill, came to visit her and found her as we have just stated. She remained this way for over forty-eight hours, without showing any sign of consciousness. She woke up without realizing the duration of her sleep and, although very weak, returned to her duties without taking drink or any food."

Sister Mary Martha, although losing awareness of her surroundings, did not usually succumb to weakness as we have just recounted... She remained, ordinarily, motionless and kneeling at the foot of the Blessed Sacrament for hours or entire nights.

On one feast day, being pressed for time with her work, she asked a Sister to take her place before the Most Blessed Sacrament for adoration, but Our Lord objected. He said: "I will not suffer another coming here to take your place."

She immediately yielded to the invitation, profoundly humbled herself, and enumerated all the petitions she had entrusted to Him: the needs of Holy Church, those of the Community, the harvest, etc. "Now," Jesus said to her, "I have heard everything, come take your rest close to Me." At that very moment our Sister lost herself in God, remaining on her knees motionless for an hour. She was this way in the students' seating area when the students entered the choir for the sermon. The Sister Sacristan then said to her: "Are you forgetting that you mustn't stay in the middle of the choir when the Community is doing its exercises here? The students are coming in."

Sister Mary Martha, still lost in God, withdrew to her place. A shake from a Sister who was passing by brought her back to the things of this world. "She had," she later said, "such a great need to remain with her Jesus!" After this grace, it was very hard for her to resume her material work.

"On July 2, 1882, our little Sister remained in the choir in ecstasy from five o'clock to seven o'clock in the evening. She was oblivious to the sermon, to the benediction of the Most Blessed Sacrament, and to the exit of the Community and Boarding School."

One Sunday in September 1887, the Holy Infant Jesus having given her a glimpse of Heaven, Vespers concluded without the blessed Seer coming back to earth. As she had to carry the cross in the procession, our Lay Sisters prodded her multiple times to get her to come back to her senses. But she was still so absorbed in God that she could not walk and had no bodily strength. She wanted to have one of her companions take the cross instead. Jesus objected: "My Bride, should it be said that you had Me carried by another after the graces I just gave you?"

"Oh, Lord, give me the strength!" Immediately, her strength returned, and she effortlessly fulfilled her consoling duty.

At the following recreation, our Sisters had lots of questions for her: "How is it you lose yourself like that?", "What are you seeing?", etc. It was a little war that filled the poor girl with confusion…

We cannot multiply the accounts. But similar incidents recurred frequently, traces of which have been continually encountered in the course of this book.

How many hours our Sister spent this way, her hands joined together and her eyes closed, without even coughing during the peak of her worst colds, not moving any more than a corpse! Sometimes during boarding school vacations or retreats, she was found in the choir at one o'clock in the afternoon with her veil still lowered,[6] continuing her thanksgiving for Holy Communion… or on Christmas morning, having been confined there since after midnight Mass.[7]

There were several times that our now deceased Mother Jeanne-Françoise Breton had approached and taken the blessed ecstatic's hands into her own. "Her hands had this something about them that was incorporeal," she said. "Contact with them compelled respect, permeating one's entire being and penetrating it with a profound impression of the supernatural. It was like coming into contact with the Beyond."

Two of our Sisters, intrigued by these long sessions, wanted to apply the same test to which the Seer of Lourdes [St.

---

[6] It is the Sisters' custom to lower their veils when going to the Holy Table and to keep them lowered until the Last Gospel at the end of Mass.

[7] The Sister in charge of closing the choir was told not to be concerned about Sister Mary Martha's presence. It was understood that she had permission to be there.

Bernadette] was subjected. One day when they found Sister Mary Martha in ecstasy in the tribune for the sick, they took the liberty of putting a lighted candle close to her joined hands until it burned her. She did not make the slightest movement that would betray any pain.

Another Sister stuck a pin sufficiently deep into her fingers. Sister Mary Martha remained equally insensitive.

Only the word "obedience" summoned our Sister back to herself. She seemed at such times to be returning from a far-off place, would get up with a bit of a stagger, and went with docility to do what she was ordered.

In response to her spiritual helper who asked her during a conversation, "Sister Mary Martha, how is it that the little Jesus sometimes keeps you in the choir for the entire morning and then, at other times, lets you leave?" she said, "Well, you see, Sister, when I am not needed and I have nothing to do, I do not know how it happens then, but I let myself free. So, there is nothing else, there is no more time... We are there together... We are happy!"

To another Sister who questioned her about the secret of these long sessions in the choir, Sister Mary Martha one day responded: "Sister, I sleep..."

It really was, in fact, the Bride's mystical slumber.

# CHAPTER 28

## DESIRE FOR HEAVEN

AND now, it is to Heaven, at Jesus's beckoning, that we shall, with Sister Mary Martha, lift the eyes of our soul.

Her soul lived far more in Heaven than on earth: her faith made it visible to her; hope and love inflamed her desires. And that is why, whether amidst sufferings or joys, whether in the course of her personal sanctification or in the course of her hidden apostolate, her life was constantly and totally oriented towards Heaven. To go to Heaven by opening it to souls through the Holy Wounds—this was her entire program.

This is how Sister Mary Martha has appeared to us up to this point. This is how she appears to us even more when we examine certain pages of the manuscripts more closely. We find recorded therein, as coming from Our Lord, beautiful and powerful reflections on Eternity.

We witness therein visions of the glorious Hereafter.

We notice therein the thirsting desire for the Heavenly Homeland, and already an anticipated communion with the happiness of the Elect.

"The earth is nothing, My daughter," the Lord Jesus said to His Bride, "the entire earth is but nothing... Look to Heaven! Heaven alone is worthy of your desires!...

"Remember your dwelling place and do not forget that you belong to Heaven's great family. You must always have your eyes on your nothingness and your heart in Heaven."

Enlightening His Servant about the last things, He moved her one day with the spectacle of the separation of soul and body: "The soul returns to God Who is its principle. The body returns also to its principle, which is the earth. This body will become glorious at the general resurrection only in virtue of the merits of the Sacred Humanity of Our Lord Jesus Christ.

"At that time, I shall resurrect it through My omnipotence and souls shall enjoy sharing their happiness with the inseparable companions of their poor earthly life...

"You do not have as much of a celebration on the day of your death! It is on that day that you shall reap what you have sown."

Did Sister Mary Martha sometimes experience a foretaste of this happiness in Heaven? Was she given a glimpse of these splendors? The manuscripts affirm this in multiple places. Her Superior wrote: "She then loses herself in amazement at the sight of such beauty!... at the sight of the great goods that the Elect possess. She participates in some manner in their happiness... her soul truly tastes some portion of Heaven's joys! She is entirely filled with them, but has only silence in the face of such wonders; the radiant expression of her face alone speaks for her and betrays this indescribable enjoyment that nothing on earth can express."

We read further in the manuscript that, on February 27, 1873, Jesus Crucified appeared in His glory amidst virginal souls, whom He pointed out to His Bride as He named them. Then our blessed Privileged One saw "the base of Mary's throne," surrounded by a multitude of Virgins. It was not permitted, on that day, for her mortal eyes to see higher, not even to glimpse the feet of our Immaculate Queen. She only saw the pedestal of her throne. "But this pedestal already had something so beautiful, so transparent and bright," that she could find nothing with which to liken it, everything else appearing dull when compared to this whiteness.

It is time to recall the nights of adoration that Sister Mary Martha sometimes spent entirely in elevations and visions of this kind: "At such times," she said, "I cannot pray, I can only contemplate and enjoy."

Sister Mary Martha did not always have the impression that her spirit was taken up into the heights; it sometimes seemed to her that Heaven came down to earth.

Sometimes Jesus presented Himself alone: just as stars hide in the presence of the sun, so did the elect disappear to make way for their King to speak familiarly with His Beloved.

Sometimes He appeared surrounded by His court. Thus, "April 4, 1869 was a day of delights for our child," the manuscript states. The Infant Jesus came to visit her with a retinue of Saints, the most distinguished among them being the Holy Founders of the Visitation, St. Bernard, St. Clare, etc.... Each one told her his or her name, and Sister Mary Martha spoke with them very simply like a child."

The Elect maintained intimate and touching relations with their protégée, especially on their feast days. Thus, on October 4, 1867, St. Francis of Assisi, appearing to her in glory "like a living copy of Our Lord," encouraged her to contemplate within herself the Wounds of her crucified Spouse.

As for the Visitation Sisters in Heaven, we know that she often enjoyed conversing with them. The religious of our Community, blessed beneficiaries of the Holy Wounds devotion and of their little Sister's immolations, were pleased to make their happiness known to her: "I had chosen Jesus as the sole object of my love," one of them said. "It was He Who was all of my perfection, it is He Who is my crown."

Jesus, Crown of Virgins, and Jesus, Crown of All the Saints, after having been "the object of their love" on earth—this was, in short, the beheld reality that so many times plunged Sister Mary Martha into rapture.

Thus, we can imagine that, as the hart panting for fountains of water, she was ever more thirsting for Heaven!

Our Sister St. Margaret Mary Alacoque one day declared to her humble emulator on earth: "Your martyrdom, for your entire life, will be the fear of being deceived and the vision of Heaven often given you. These two things will make you suffer more than anything in the world!"

This was profoundly true!... Fearing being in delusion, what a cruel affliction! Glimpsing Heaven yet remaining here below, what a martyrdom! How much our Sister suffered from these things!

"Your suffering will be being obliged to busy yourself with the things of the earth," the Divine Spouse said.

This was no less true... When this dear soul came back from Heaven, the return to external occupations weighed heavily upon her, so much did she languish with desire for the Everlasting Hills!

"What do You gain, Good Master," she sighed, "by letting me live any longer?" And even: "Good Master, take me."

In response to these supplications, Jesus answered: "My daughter, you must still remain. I am going to prepare your place.

"I still have things to reveal to you... When everything is accomplished in you, I shall take you... The illness that will cause your death will come from My Wounds."

... And Sister Mary Martha waited, in resignation, as she daily fulfilled her "task" and God's good pleasure.

# CHAPTER 29

## FINAL YEARS AND DEATH
## OF SISTER MARY MARTHA

T HE year 1887 ended in our monastery with a very painful sacrifice.

Having been ill for a month with bronchitis, which had given us serious concerns, our Very Honorable Mother Thérèse-Eugénie Revel seemed to be recovering when the rheumatism from which she had been suffering for a long time suddenly spread to her heart—the danger became imminent and the Last Sacraments had to be administered. On the morning of December 30, before the Community could even be brought together, Her Charity was taken from us almost abruptly; some Sisters, sobbing, had scarcely surrounded the bed where she lay; the others hurried to this desolate cry: "Our Mother has died!"

On January 4, 1888, God gave our mourning family as a consoling angel our Very Honorable Mother Jeanne-Marie-Anne Spinella, a former novitiate companion of good Sister Mary Martha. Six years later, in 1894, our Very Honorable Mother Jeanne-Françoise Breton succeeded her in office, and from then until 1917, these two now deceased Mothers alternated in governing the Community.

Our Lord did not permit Sister Mary Martha's new Superiors to have an exact knowledge of the graces with which He filled His Servant.

Regarding the notebooks as a deposition of conscience containing information given in confidence, our Very Honorable Sister and former Mother Marie-Alexis Blanc handed them over after the death of our Mother Thérèse-Eugénie to Father Collonge, our new Chaplain, and it was in his custody that they were to remain until the death of the Lord's Privileged One.

The venerable Sister Marie-Alexis died subsequently in 1893. One of our Lay Sister's consolations had been to bestow many kind attentions for a few years on the one who was her last confidante and whose death was to seal the divine favors in secrecy for a long time.

Sister Mary Martha, ordinarily so emotional on these occasions of mourning, was completely serene in her personal conviction concerning the eternal happiness of the former Mother, over whom we were grieving. She asserted that "we had not lost her." She was so certain at the time that one of our Sisters asked her one day, "But really, tell me, have you seen her?"

"Well, yes!" she admitted. And pointing to a space in her little area, she added, "I saw her there, but you will know nothing more about it."

Our dear Sister was approaching her fifty-second year of age. A new phase of her life was beginning.

In response to her earnest request, and in return for her generous acquiescence to the death of our two Superiors, Our Lord had promised her silence concerning the favors with which He filled her, and that an ever more impenetrable veil would keep her hidden. During this final period, nothing of the extraordinary graces with which she was favored appeared on the exterior—nothing except the long hours during which the pious Lay Sister remained before the Most Blessed Sacrament, motionless and unresponsive as in ecstasy.

Continual prayer, work, mortification, silence, and absolute self-effacement—such was her life. But during this time, like the mustard seed thrown onto the ground, the Holy Wounds devotion was starting to grow in people's hearts.

At this point, we shall defer to our Very Honorable Mother Jeanne-Françoise Breton. Almost all of the following details are taken from the unpublished summary *The Life of Sister Mary Martha* by this now deceased Mother who was with the Servant of God during her final struggle and witnessed her last breath.

"Shortly after our first election (1894), this good Sister respectfully and humbly approached us and said: 'Mother, the good God says that He can make a Superior out of a dry stick.' We could not help smiling at this unexpected encouragement, which was so welcome at the time, and admiring the perfect simplicity with which it was communicated to us."

When the boarding school disappeared in 1904, it was a blow to our good late Sister. For close to forty years she had exerted all her strength and dedication in the service of "our children." She missed our children!

Moreover, the earth was so sad, and her Good Master appeared to her to be so offended!

The moving of our exiled Sisters, the threats under which we ourselves lived, and the preparations that had to be made in the monastery in light of a potential departure broke her heart, all the more so because Jesus remained silent to all her petitions.

When we pressed her to tell us if she knew anything of Providence's designs in our respect, she had only this to say: "He says nothing!" What was the meaning of this silence, to which the Good Master had so little accustomed her? Now knowing of all the assurances given at other times to our

Mothers, and also of the threats to not hold to His promises "if love should slacken," we understand the anxiety that gripped our dear Sister's heart... She thus redoubled her fidelity to "her task," that is to say to offering up the Divine Wounds of Jesus for the Community and for souls. Up until her death, in her final years especially, her entire spiritual life seemed to come down to this. "I have done my task," she would say each time she rendered an account.

Sister Mary Martha aged much during this time, but she did not slacken in her zeal for prayer or work despite growing infirmities.

It took courage for her to see her work through to completion, even for simple tasks such as sweeping, picking vegetables and fruit, etc. But Our Lord continued to bless everything entrusted to her. The strawberry plants, among other things, were astonishingly fruitful. When the closing of the boarding school forced us to seek means in our enclosure's produce, "Sister Mary Martha's strawberries" were very appreciated.

As early as four o'clock in the morning, she could be seen bending to the ground, despite her swollen, rheumatic legs, to pick these beautiful, good strawberries, an enormous quantity of which she would deliver to our Sister Bursar before six o'clock. The friends to whom they were sold found them to have an exquisite wild strawberry taste... Was this exceptional flavor left by her little Divine Helper?... We do not know. But what is certain is that she was sometimes heard conversing with an invisible being, and that the extraordinary, even religious, care she put into her harvesting indeed proved that she saw each fruit as a gift from God.

The Divine Bridegroom was preparing to soon crown His humble Bride.

During the great drought of 1906, our Sister seemed as though crushed beneath the weight of God's justice: "The good God is very unhappy, He is very angry," she confided to our Very Honorable Sister Assistant. "Do you not see how He is punishing?... Oh, how angry He is at men!... They are doing so much evil!"

The Sister Assistant replied, "Your Charity always sees Our Lord irritated... but is He not above all good and merciful?"

"Oh, yes, He is good... but He is so much offended!... Our Lord has suffered so much for them; now, he punishes. I always pray that He pardons, but I am not enough... everyone would need to pray..."

Poor dear Sister! She spoke truly. Her life was nothing but a prayer and, despite the weariness of old age, it was more often than not with her arms outstretched in the form of a cross that we saw her, after her days of toil, making the Way of the Cross and offering the Holy Wounds for the salvation of the world.

During the final Christmas night she spent on earth, it seems Jesus warned her of her approaching departure from this world, and, at the same time, of the sufferings He wanted to still ask of her.

One Sister who was close to her during midnight Mass heard her cry out in anguish: "O my Jesus, not that!... Everything, yes everything, but not that!"

"That" must have been the difficult and painful illness... "That" must have been foremost the interior abandonment, the absence of the Beloved Savior... She who was used to His dear presence and His daily conversation could not accept being deprived of this without dreadful heartbreak!

Thus, from that day forward, we noticed that a deep sadness had impressed itself on her countenance.

Her strength visibly deteriorated, and one would have believed her much older than she was. Winter was very cold. However, accustomed to regarding her own miseries as nothing, she always went outside, although her legs were considerably swollen and a bad cold tired her day and night. This was so ordinary for her in the winter season that we did not think of frightening ourselves about it. The best remedy, according to her, was to go through the garden, even when snow-covered, in search of some edible plant.

But there came a time when, the suffering ever increasing, she had to stay in the infirmary. The doctor detected a case of albuminuria with serious complications. Beginning on the following day, February 13, 1907, she sensed that her end was coming and asked for the Last Sacraments.

There still remained a sorrowful Calvary for her to climb: five weeks of extreme purifications during which her Savior united her more than ever to the physical and spiritual agonies of His Passion.

Swelling and shortness of breath left her in an unbearable state. The remedies prescribed to prolong her life only served to increase her sufferings, all while she seemed to be beset by an interior abandonment that was more difficult and more prolonged than she had ever known.

Spiritual graces, however, were outwardly lavished upon her. Her good Master deigned each morning to come strengthen her in Holy Communion... Each evening she was paid a paternal visit by our priest confessor, whom she received with gratitude. These helps were very necessary for her, as the extent to which

God permitted her to be reduced to suffering and abjection was incredible...

We sensed there was something mysterious in this last of nature's struggles. It would not be difficult for us to believe that there was a kind of return of the diabolical attacks that she had suffered so much in times past.

A sorrowful silence hovered about this dear sick one. Any communication she might have had with those who came to watch over her and visit her was scarce. The desire for death seemed very far from her heart, for she dismissed anything that might bring it to mind...

Her silence soon became a kind of semi-somnolence. Sister Marie-Jacqueline, her twin in profession and an assistant at the infirmary, spent all her days close to her, at least inasmuch as her own infirmities permitted, surrounding her with devoted care when the Officer had to go away.

Every morning, we went to see whether she was capable of receiving Holy Communion. Several times during the final week she had to go without it... What was taking place between her soul and Jesus?... No one was privy to the secret. Was not her good Master, after having continuously united her to His own Passion, completing in her the likeness to His death? Perhaps He was multiplying her sufferings for all those among us whom she was to still help to sooner enjoy God through the merits of the Holy Wounds, and for those poor sinners and suffering souls for whom she had given and sacrificed her entire life.

This Victim's last three days were heartbreaking. Unceasingly she called out to Our Lord: "My All! My All!... Come! Come! But come quickly!"

For some time, the overall swelling forced her to remain in an armchair. She had to be fastened to it since she kept sliding forward. It was a pity to see her that way, without a minute of rest day or night.

Her Beloved still came to visit her, but she did not cease imploring Him, even at the time of thanksgiving: "My Beloved!... My Beloved!" Was He then keeping hidden from her His Sacred Humanity which, since her childhood, she had contemplated in all her communions? Or did this momentary gift only intensify a hunger for God that only her eternal possession of Him could satisfy? God only knows.

She ended up being placed on a simple straw mattress, and from that point forward she was able to rest a bit.

The night of Wednesday, March 20 to Thursday, March 21 was terrible. Unremitting cries of "Mother, help, help!" were heartbreaking to all. They did not cease until morning. We remained convinced that, in this final battle with the enemy, our good heavenly Mother had finally made her victorious.

This good Mother, on the First Vespers of her Compassion,[1] was to come for the privileged child whom she had taught to love Jesus Crucified.

Our Chaplain repeated several times to the dear dying one the grace of holy absolution and prayers commending her soul. She gave no sign of consciousness; but on her features, which were previously gripped by suffering and anguish, pervaded little by little the calm of eternal rest.

---

[1] In 1907, the feast of Our Lady of Compassion, traditionally celebrated on the Friday preceding Palm Sunday, fell on March 22. First Vespers for the feast therefore took place on the evening of Thursday, March 21.—Trans.

It was a spectacle not lacking in grandeur. It evoked the memory of deaths depicted in certain paintings: those of St. Louis and St. Francis Xavier, for example, expiring on a mean bed or a bed of ashes.

All of us surrounded her with our presence and our prayers.

Thousands of times, perhaps, the Community recited this invocation: "My Jesus, pardon and mercy through the merits of Thy Holy Wounds." It was the same invocation she had repeated so many times for our dying Sisters!

Were those dear deceased ones and venerable Mothers who had preceded her to the Homeland not invisibly present in that poor little cell?... What a beautiful procession they must have made for this humble Lay Sister upon her entrance into Heaven!

At around eight o'clock in the evening her final breath came so peacefully that we were unable to perceive it... And as we continued to surround the virginal body with our prayers, the heavenly abode witnessed—so we like to believe—the fulfillment of one of the visions that had gladdened the heart of Sister Mary Martha in the days of her youth. Her soul found itself taken up into Paradise. The Blessed, making space in their ranks, let her pass to go very close to Our Lord, and they sang in unison with a ravishing voice: "The one who was the littlest shall become the greatest."

*And He hath exalted the humble!*

# CHAPTER 30

## AFTER DEATH

truly extraordinary air of youthfulness spread over Sister Mary Martha's features shortly after her passing. They took on a distinction and a nobility that they were far from having during her life. No trace of corruption appeared on this body that had been marked for several days with livid patches of gangrene.

Following the Order's custom, our dear Sister was clothed in the religious habit and a crown of white roses was placed over the black veil.[1] In anticipation of the future, the Deceased's identifying information, enclosed by the Very Honorable Mother Jeanne-Françoise Breton in an iron box sealed with the seal of our monastery, was placed on her body.

In the open casket which was surrounded with white flowers, the Servant of God remained exposed in the choir until the time for the funeral, which took place on the morning of March 23. For a number of years, we had no longer enjoyed the consolation of keeping the remains of our deceased Sisters in our little cemetery. Thus, it was with emotion that we witnessed the venerated casket pass outside the cloister door and the funeral ceremony take place in our exterior chapel.[2]

---

[1] The white veil, which our lay sisters' work requires, is replaced after death with the black veil the choir sisters receive at profession.

[2] Fr. C., who as parish vicar was present at Sister Mary Martha's funeral, remembered the words spoken to him at the time by Fr. Collonge, our chaplain: "This Sister will one day be talked about."

Sister Mary Martha's body was buried in the city cemetery. It would remain there for ten years, until May 1917.[3] With our different burial concessions reaching their expiration, we obtained permission, at that time, to bring back to the monastery the Sisters who had died since 1901.

The Servant of God's coffin, which had been put in a damp place, was just about consumed, as was the flesh inside. The skeleton and the clothing had not undergone any notable deterioration.

An interesting detail: The body of our Sister Marie-Jacqueline, who died in 1908, was found so well intact that the gravediggers said: "It is Sister Arbet who is the saint."

The remains of Sister Mary Martha, put separately into a new coffin, were placed in our cemetery.

However, as we stated earlier, following the death of Jesus's Privileged One, the manuscripts pertaining to her graces were passed from our Chaplain's hands to those of our Very Honorable Mother Jeanne-Françoise Breton. Hardly had the latter skimmed through the first pages when she understood the value of the treasure that had been entrusted to us and felt the desire to communicate to our Institute the spiritual riches contained in these precious memoirs. Following the custom established by our Holy Founders, she thus undertook writing *The Summary of the Life and Virtues of Our Dear Sister Mary Martha Chambon*. However, as the circumstances demanded a prudent reserve, our good Mother contented herself with sending our monasteries the short obituary from the book of vows, inviting them to often repeat with us: "Lord, deign to glorify Thy

---

[3] Pious persons made it a habit to visit this modest grave and to have recourse to the Servant of God in order to obtain spiritual and temporal favors.

Servant, who glorified Thee through her humility and through her zeal in so lovingly offering up the merits of Thy Holy Wounds!"

For fifteen years, the shadow that was Sister Mary Martha's companion here below seemed to still want to envelop her. Everything about her followed a slow progression until the day when, suddenly like lightning ripping through the sky, the Notice, which events had brought about, threw light onto the Holy Wounds devotion and the humble apostle to whom the Crucified Savior entrusted the mission of its propagation.

In 1915, we were given as superior Canon Maillet, the vicar general of the archdiocese, a distinguished casuist, a respected theologian, and, moreover, a very positive soul. Already an extraordinary confessor to the Community since 1895 and a close friend of Canon Collonge, he knew Sister Mary Martha. The summary of her life and the manuscripts having been put into his hands, he was pleased to repeat: "Everything conforms to the soundest doctrine. I have found nothing in this contrary to the teachings of the Church." And he heartily encouraged us to bring to light the story of the graces granted to our Sister. His Excellency Archbishop Castellan showed himself favorable to this plan, it being vaguely spoken of as a project, and one that would not be without difficulties.

This was as far as things were when, the discussion one day touching on the "silence" our Privileged One was keeping up above, the Very Honorable Sister Jeanne-Marie-Anne Spinella said smilingly: "When I get to Heaven, I am going to shake Sister Mary Martha up!" This was in 1922, a few weeks prior to her death. As a matter of fact, shortly after her death, our Very Honorable Mother felt a strong inspiration to carry out one of the last wishes of this dearly departed one: the request to extend to the entire world the indulgence tied to the Holy Wounds invocations.[4]

The steps to be taken and the need to enlighten the archdiocese's ecclesiastical superiors about the origin of the two prayers led to the writing of our Notice: *Sister Mary Martha Chambon and the Holy Wounds of Our Lord Jesus Christ.*

We stated the following at the end of the second edition: When events led us to publish these pages on December 13, 1923, we thought they would not go beyond the familial enclosures of our monasteries and the friendly network of those close to the House, and that a few hundred copies would suffice. Now, at the time of this writing, the hundreds anticipated have become hundreds of thousands if one counts the ten to twelve translations in foreign languages.

The devotion has gone outside the monasteries. It has crossed international borders and oceans. The Notice of the Holy Wounds has been spread everywhere, as have the leaflets containing the Rosary of Mercy. From everywhere rise up to Heaven invocations to the true Founts of Salvation. From everywhere go out cries of thanksgiving for the favors obtained through this holy practice.

It is a renewal of the devotion to the Savior's Passion. It is Sister Mary Martha's "mission" that is being accomplished.

Stirred up by reading the Notice, a desire has risen in pious hearts: that of knowing more of the privileged soul, an instrument of divine mercy. A unanimous sense of veneration

---

[4] Owing to the initiative of our Very Honorable Mother Jeanne-Françoise Breton, this indulgence, granted to our Community in 1909, had been subject in 1912 to the revision decreed by the Sovereign Pontiff's *motu proprio.* Answering our hearts' (unexpressed) desire, the Sacred Congregation then granted it for ten years "to the entire Visitation Order."

and confidence has also come about, piously surrounding the name of the humble lay sister.

In the face of this movement coming from the outside, how could those of us inside the monastery not be somewhat moved? The exhumation of the Servant of God's remains seemed necessary. On January 31, 1924, we found the entire closed coffin, almost all the bones, and a portion of the clothing. The iron box, which must have disappeared during the first exhumation, had left a rusty imprint that could be made out on one of the habit's sleeves. Even some pieces of wax that had sealed it were found.

After their medical examination, these bones were put into a leaded zinc chest, which, on the following February 11, was placed beneath a marble slab in the Chapel of Our Lady of the Seven Sorrows, where our dear Sister had so often knelt.[5]

Sister Mary Martha did not delay in sending us a smile from up in Heaven. On the first Friday of November 1925, one of our lay sisters, who had been wasting away for several months due to a virtual inability to take food, suddenly regained her strength and the ability to digest after a novena was made to the Servant of God.[6]

---

[5] At the time of this translation in 2019, Sister Mary Martha's remains (as well as the "miraculous Christ") are kept at the Visitation of Marclaz in Thonon-les-Bains, approximately 95 kilometers northeast of Chambéry. The Visitation Sisters left Chambéry in 1956 to relocate to Château de Menjoud in Saint-Pierre-d'Albigny (about 17 kilometers to the east). In 2005, the few Sisters remaining at Saint-Pierre-d'Albigny left to merge with the community in Thonon-les-Bains.

Incidentally, a factor in the Visitation's 1956 departure from Chambéry was the partial destruction of their monastery by an American bombardment during the Second World War, which claimed the lives of two of the Sisters. The aerial bombing occurred on the morning of May 26, 1944.—Trans.

[6] A fact to which Dr. Amédée Denarié officially attested.

It is not only in the monastery that Jesus's Privileged One manifests her power of intercession. The letters received attest to favors that appear to respond to the confidence of Sister Mary Martha's clients: consolations in suffering, graces of light and strength to understand and carry one's cross, and conversions and healings.

As a guarantee of protection and as an assurance of being more easily answered, numerous pious persons ask that their names and petitions be placed over the humble Servant of God's resting place.

As for the multiple testimonies of satisfaction that have welcomed the Notice, we shall only quote one of them, as it seems to sum up all of them and is signed with a name which death has consecrated.

*Paris, 22 September 1924*

*I am rather late in responding to the admirable booklet you sent. It is just that I wanted to read and enjoy it before thanking you.*

*The hand of God can be seen throughout these pages, which are so stripped of self.*

*This Notice is a signal blessing which opens the soul of Christ to everyone, and, for my part, I wish to keep its remembrance until my departure, until arriving where all light is consummated.*

*I admire how Our Lord keeps His mode of action within a fixed milieu. It is the same grace for St. Margaret Mary Alacoque as for the blessed Lay Sister. It is the same way of entering into contact with heavenly things, of bringing them nearer to us, and of burying ourselves in them.*

*Friar T. G. Vallée, O.P.*

**God be blessed!**

CPSIA information can be obtained
at www.ICGtesting.com
Printed in the USA
LVHW011618210119
604682LV00016B/405/P

9 781732 873407